# THE KHMERS

## HISTORY AND TREASURES OF AN ANCIENT CIVILIZATION

WHITE STAR PUBLISHERS

# CONTENTS

WHITE STAR PUBLISHERS

TEXTS
STEFANO VECCHIA

EDITORIAL DIRECTOR
VALERIA MANFERTO DE FABIANIS

COLLABORATING EDITORS
LAURA ACCOMAZZO
GIORGIO FERRERO

GRAPHIC DESIGNER
PAOLA PIACCO

WS White Star Publishers® is a registered trademark
property of De Agostini Libri S.p.A.

© 2007, 2014 De Agostini Libri S.p.A.
Via G. da Verrazano, 15
28100 Novara, Italy
www.whitestar.it - www.deagostini.it

Translation: Richard Pierce

ISBN 978-88-544-0689-6
 2 3 4 5 6   18 17 16 15 14

Printed in China

1 - AT BANTEAY SREI THERE ARE REPRESENTATIONS
OF THE EPISODES FROM THE LEGEND OF SHIVA.

2-3 - THE FOUR-HEADED TOP OF ONE OF THE TOWERS
OF THE BAYON MANIFESTS THE OMNISCIENT NATURE OF
THE BODHISATTVA AVALOKISTESHVARA AND OF THE KING.

4-5 - THE RELATIVELY SMALL BANTEAY SREI IS
STRIKING WITH ITS DECORATION, WHICH FOR THE MOST
PART DREW INSPIRATION FROM THE HINDU EPICS.

6-7 - THE JUDGMENT OF THE DEAD IS DEPICTED
ON A WALL OF THE THIRD GALLERY AT ANGKOR WAT.

9 - THIS BUDDHA (H. 43 IN.) , EXECUTED IN THE
TYPICAL BAYON STYLE, WAS DISCOVERED IN THE PREAH
KHAN COMPLEX (MUSÉE GUIMET, PARIS).

In January 1860, the French naturalist Henry Mouhot was overwhelmed by the walls decorated with enigmatic faces and by the first elements of an otherworldly architecture that he came upon, for the first time in centuries penetrating the silence and mystery of the Bayon at Angkor Thom. Around him was a dense jungle that concealed grandiose ruins and a legend that had been handed down by generations of farmers, religious leaders and monks. Thus was reborn the grandeur of Angkor–which had never been totally obliterated–and of the empire whose capital it had been for 500 years. Certainly, Mouhot was not the first Westerner to venture into the jungle north of the Great Lake in Cambodia that had become a vast muddy area during the monsoon season. But he was the one who paved the way for a long list of archaeologists, adventurers and plunderers–serious scholars and restorers as well as charlatans–who contributed to our knowledge of a great civilization. And he also opened the door to the modern flow of visitors, that in certain respects—given the characteristics and intrinsic fragility of the ruins of Angkor—could be called "mass tourism", and as such can be considered both an important economic resource and a serious problem.

Present-day Cambodia, which rightly considers itself the heir of the great Khmer empire, is a small nation that combines a rich and enviable ancient history with a recent past that was one of the most turbulent in all Asia. The history of this nation was cancelled by the Khmer Rouge regime (1975-1978) in an insane attempt to remove all traces of the past and build a new society from nothing; it was therefore imperative, after such a cruel and dramatic period, that Cambo-

dia find its roots in its former grandeur and then struggle to build its future upon it. The Cambodians had never really lost sight of or forgotten their glorious heritage, since the basis for this identity was favored by their extraordinary ethnic homogeneity: 90% of today's 10,000,000 or so Cambodians belong to the Khmer ethnic group. This amazing predominance dates from long ago, from the empire that from the 9th to the 15th century controlled most of Indochina and to this day is an indispensable reference point for the Khmer civilization and the Cambodian nation, as well as for all Southeast Asia, for that matter. However, there are vast zones still wrapped in mystery, which archaeology and the study of comparative civilizations cannot shed much light on. There are extensive areas of obscurity concerning the initial phases of its history, the role played therein by the Hindu-Buddhist civilization centered in Sumatra and Java, and the true origins of the small principalities that in the 7th century began to be united into a single, albeit basically unstable, Khmer power. For example, archaeological finds and indirect documentation have shown that the ancient indigenous civilization was predominantly urban and as such influenced the architecture and art of a huge continental region. And yet–and this is only one of the contradictions that the many mysteries of the Angkor civilization have perpetuated–the present-day Khmer still consider themselves members of an agricultural civilization, whose existence and survival are based on the rhythm of the cultivation, in flooded fields, of rice; which is not only the staple of these people, but also the symbol of the human condition, with its cycles, successes and disasters. Thus we have a rural concept of society, with its ad-

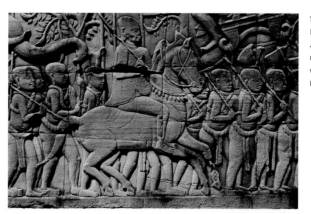

10 - DETAIL OF A BAS-
RELIEF IN THE OUTER
GALLERY OF THE BAYON,
DEPICTING A MILITARY
PARADE.

11 - THE TOWERS OF THE
BAYON, AT ANGKOR THOM,
ARE DECORATED WITH
FACES OF LOKESHVARA,
WHICH ACTUALLY PORTRAY
KING JAYAVARMAN VII.

miration of the values and rhythms of the countryside and its rejection of the city and the alien and antagonistic features it represents. The Khmer kingdom, which in certain periods had the territorial dimension and features of a true empire, distinguished itself once again from the Asiatic context, in which the possibility of dominion was always guaranteed more by the capacity to assimilate the conquered peoples and integrate them into one's own culture than by sheer military power; it always imposed itself on others as the only possible model, which one had to accept and submit to totally, the only alternative being annihilation.

A major role in the definition of Khmer power was also played by its location (or better, the location of its fulcrum, Angkor) in an area that was basically marginal within the context of continental Asia and decentralized with respect to the traditional major routes of trade, pilgrimage and conquest. In the light of dramatic historic evolutions, climatic changes and alterations to the water supply system and the water cycle, it is difficult nowadays to say whether the decision to choose the plain around the northern course of the Tonlé Sap River in Cambodia as the center of the new Khmer power was made solely for defensive, political or material reasons, or rather for a combination of these factors. Little is known of the role played by geomancy, by the management of concepts that had existed before the rise of Hinduism and, later, Buddhism as the state religion, and of sites in which beliefs, myths and energy were concentrated and spread, and it has been investigated even less, but it was probably important in the past, just as it still important in the life of Cambodians today. Certainly, the particular concept of power among the Khmer, and its religious derivation or inspiration, is a very important and extremely interesting subject that must be studied and discussed.

Surely, part of the reason for the centuries-old oblivion

of Khmer civilization was the situation created by the crisis of the empire. For centuries the territory of present-day Cambodia had to endure the presence of two antagonistic neighbors: Thailand (known as Siam in the past) and Vietnam. The Siamese caused the definitive downfall of Angkor at the end of the 15th century, and from that time to the French annexation of Cambodia in 1863, the city remained under Siamese dominion. Again, for a brief period during World War II, the Siamese took over the northern provinces of Siem Reap and Battambang, where the most important Khmer archaeological sites are situated (in fact, Siem Reap, which significantly enough means "conquered by Siam," is the location of the principal centers of Khmer civilization).

Today, a new awareness of the value of their past is taking hold among the Cambodians and Angkor is gradually emerging as the symbol of a cultural heritage that the present-day Khmer can acknowledge as their very own, exclusive and at the same time universal. This recognition and sense of belonging is to be seen in the national flag, which contains the towers of Angkok Wat. Yet everyone is well aware of the fact that the price to be paid for the new materialism and various imported cultural influences is and will be quite heavy.

The aim of this book is to outline the evolution and background of one of the most splendid and long-lived civilizations in all Asia. Ranging from the classical studies to the most recent theories, it is for all those who wish to know the basic facts of the Khmer culture—leaving aside all romantic notions and stereotypes—and is presented in a simple, engaging manner. The objective is not only to illustrate what has contributed to creating the fascination of a great civilization, but also to stimulate and encourage further study and, why not? more direct knowledge.

13 - THIS SANDSTONE HEAD (H. 16 IN.)
DEPICTS JAYAVARMAN VII, THE GREAT
KHMER KING WHO BUILT THE CITY OF
ANGKOR THOM, WHICH MARKED THE
APOGEE OF KHMER ART AND
ARCHITECTURE (NATIONAL MUSEUM,
PHNOM PENH).

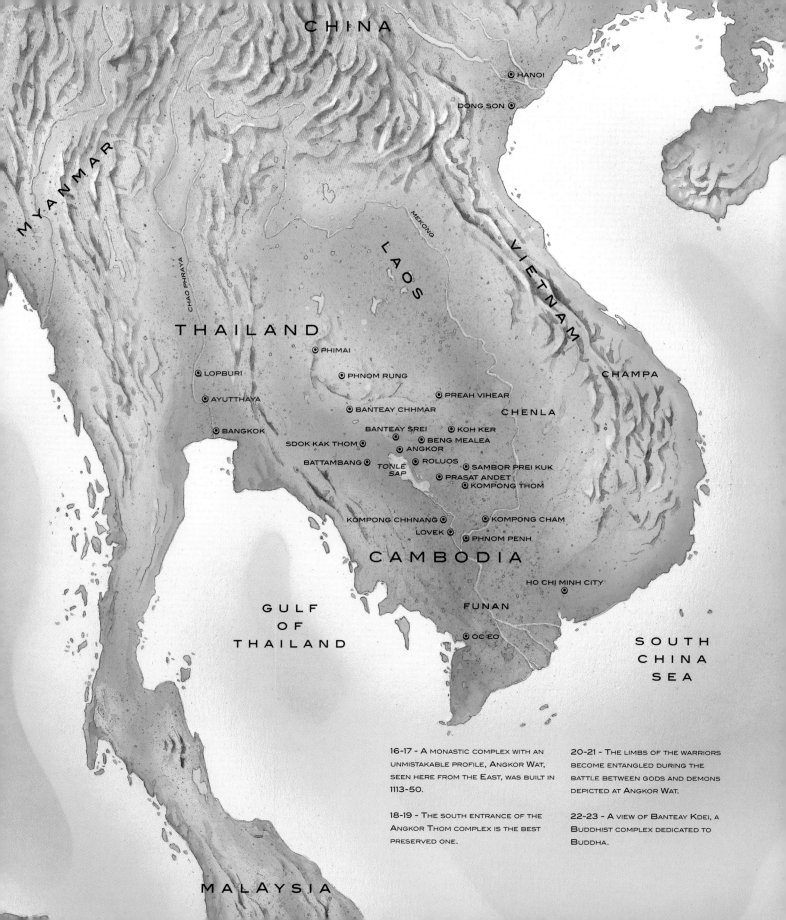

CHINA

⊙ HANOI

DONG SON ⊙

MYANMAR

MEKONG

LAOS

VIETNAM

CHAO PHRAYA

THAILAND

⊙ PHIMAI

⊙ LOPBURI

⊙ PHNOM RUNG

CHAMPA

⊙ AYUTTHAYA

⊙ PREAH VIHEAR

CHENLA

⊙ BANTEAY CHHMAR

BANTEAY SREI ⊙    ⊙ KOH KER

⊙ BANGKOK

SDOK KAK THOM ⊙    ⊙ BENG MEALEA

⊙ ANGKOR

BATTAMBANG ⊙    ⊙ ROLUOS    ⊙ SAMBOR PREI KUK

TONLÉ
SAP

⊙ PRASAT ANDET
⊙ KOMPONG THOM

KOMPONG CHHNANG ⊙    ⊙ KOMPONG CHAM

LOVEK ⊙

⊙ PHNOM PENH

CAMBODIA

HO CHI MINH CITY ⊙

GULF
OF
THAILAND

FUNAN

SOUTH
CHINA
SEA

⊙ OC EO

MALAYSIA

16-17 - A monastic complex with an unmistakable profile, Angkor Wat, seen here from the East, was built in 1113-50.

18-19 - The south entrance of the Angkor Thom complex is the best preserved one.

20-21 - The limbs of the warriors become entangled during the battle between gods and demons depicted at Angkor Wat.

22-23 - A view of Banteay Kdei, a Buddhist complex dedicated to Buddha.

## THE PROTO-HISTORIC PERIOD

### (6th-2nd century BC)

At the end of the Iron Age, the region that was later to be under Khmer dominion witnessed the rise of small principalities and a great many cities, especially along the banks of the Tonlé Sap and Mekong rivers. Gradually, as navigation techniques improved, the coasts of Cambodia and Vietnam became part of the trade routes that started off in Rome and the Middle East and went as far as India and China. Pilgrims and merchants settled in the territory of present-day Cambodia and along the lower course of the Mekong River, bringing with them heterogeneous cultural and religious elements and practices, particularly those of Indian origin.

## THE PRE-ANGKOR PERIOD

### (1st-8th century AD)

This period witnessed the rise of Funan, a commercial confederation centered in the Mekong Delta, which for a long time extended its influence over southern Cambodia. At a later stage (but scholars are still disputing the dates of the historic events of Funan, and there is little historic documentation in this regard) a scission in the confederation brought about the birth of Chenla, which was probably another union of city-states and commercial ports of call. The first sculpture of Buddhist and Hindu inspiration dates from this period. Subsequently the Indian and Hindu influence became more and more concrete, affecting not only the local religion but every facet of social life as well, including religious architecture and art. Military campaigns, which were of limited territorial scope but had considerable cultural impact, came from the Indonesian empire of Srivijaya, undermining the power of Chenla. The Khmer clans took advantage of this situation, gaining increasingly larger territories and independence, especially in central-northern Cambodia.

## THE ANGKOR PERIOD

### (9th-13th century)

In the year 802, in a ceremony officiated by Brahmins on the Phnom Kulen, Jayavarman II, a figure who in many respects is still obscure but was certainly influenced by Javanese culture and the Hindu religion, became the king of the Khmers of the future Angkor. With his coronation two features of Khmer rulers became prominent: his role as both *chakravartin* (universal sovereign) on a political level and *devaraja* (god-king) on a religious and dynastic plane. To date, no inscription has been found that dates from his reign, and the main source of information concerning this king is the stele of Sdok Kak Thom, which was carved a few centuries after his death. Under Jayavarman II and then for centuries to come, the state religion was Mahayana Buddhism, but the divinities of the Hindu pantheon were worshipped and became the center of cults. Jayavarman founded Hariharalaya, near what was to become Angkor, but the eminently urban characteristics of the Khmer civilization were better defined under his successors. Yashovarman I founded Angkor (in the East Baray area). Suryavarman II had Angkor Wat built in 1130-50. In 1177 the Cham, whose kingdom originated in central-southern Vietnam, sacked Angkor. During the reign of Jayavarman VIII the Khmer empire achieved its maximum extension. A new capital, Angkor Thom, was founded, and the Bayon was built inside it.

## CRISIS: THE POST-CLASSICAL PERIOD

### (13th-15th century)

Repeated invasions on the part of the Thai weakened the political and military power of the Khmer empire, and Theravada Buddhism became the state religion. Pali, the language of the Theravada canon, replaced Sanskrit as the official language of Buddhist texts. From 1309 to 1431, during the reign of weak kings who gradually lost more and more of their territory, Angkor was sacked several times. The year 1431 marked the last major invasion on the part of the Thai, who conquered Angkor and pillaged most of its works of art, taking them to their capital, Ayutthaya.

## DECADENCE AND REVIVAL

### (16th-19th century)

In 1528, after decades of instability and the gradual loss of the territory under the control of Angkor, King Ang Chan I moved his capital further south, to Lovek. Later, partly due to dynastic struggles, Phnom Penh took on greater importance, eventually becoming the capital of what remained of the Khmer empire. Angkor and the other main Khmer cities gradually became depopulated. The Buddhist monastic communities are to be credited for preserving the memory of these cities; indeed, in some cases they even maintained them physically, since they lived in them for centuries. The 'rediscovery' of Angkor (which was preceded by several reports made to the French colonial authorities) took place in January 1860, when the French naturalist Henry Mouhot found the ruins of Angkor Thom in the midst of the forest and explored it for three weeks. This event, together with the accounts of other travelers, led to the June 1866 French archaeological expedition at Angkor and to the beginning of restoration and preservation work that that has never been interrupted, except for the period when the Khmer Rouge were in power (1975-78).

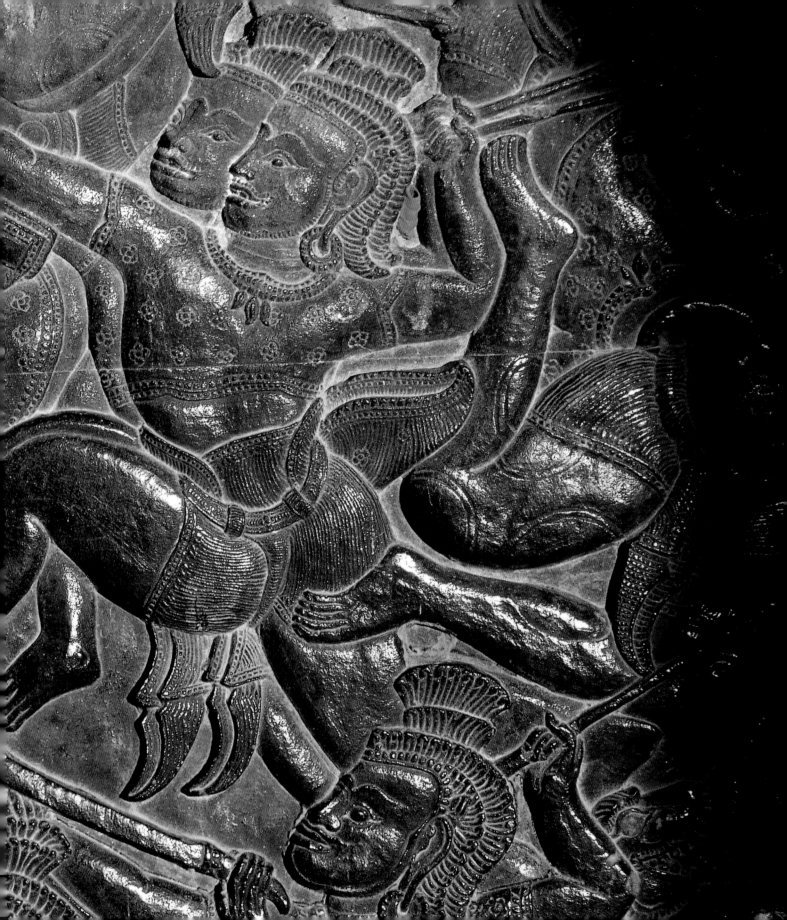

# 1

# THE ORIGINS

# THE PREHISTORY OF THE REGION

Very little is known about the most ancient history of the Cambodia region, which depended (and still depends) on the cyclical rainfall that enriches its soil but also makes the life of the inhabitants very unstable. The oldest known settlement, Loang Spean, in the province of Battambang, dates to the VI Millennium BC: a network of caverns where the population produced vases with corded and combed motifs as well as tools made of smoothed stone. The other sites, which reveal different degrees of evolution, date from the 15th to the 2nd century BC. The continuous efforts made to manage the water resources in a positive and beneficial manner–the potentially devastating monsoon rains that to this day claim victims every year and force part of the population to temporarily migrate to safer areas–has been a constant factor in local history. All this leads one to believe that the ancestors of the Khmer were also greatly influenced by these circumstances, which by no means favored either a sedentary lifestyle or the production and development of complex and large-scale handicrafts.

However, archaeological finds, especially drums, bells, and everyday ornaments and objects made of bronze, along with stone artifacts with inscriptions, all bear witness to the presence and duration of the Bronze Age in the Cambodia region, which in any case dates from before the 1st century BC. Most of these finds come from the archaeological sites of Samraong Saen and Anlung Phdao, in the Kompong Chhnang province, Kbal Romeah in the province of Preah Vihear, La-ang Spean in the province of Battambang, Srae Sbauv and Phnom Roluoch in the Kracheh province, and Memut in the province of Kompong Cham. Therefore they are all outside of the provenance of the later Khmer civilization. Yet one cannot help thinking that, as the entire Indochinese region has since most ancient times shared activities essential to the survival of human communities such as the cultivation of rice, the domestication of oxen and water buffaloes, and the use of metal, and has engaged in similar animistic rituals, part of the legacy of

Angkor must have derived from earlier traditions as well as from outside influences.

From the very beginning of its history the region that would later become the center of Khmer power felt the strong and permanent influence of Indian civilization, which covered a much vaster territory, ranging from Burma to the periphery of the Chinese empire and from Tibet to the Malaysian-Indonesian archipelago. The most long-lasting influence was certainly religious, which had the two-fold and often complementary imprint of Buddhism and Hinduism, but this was associated with a marked cultural configuration deriving from the patronage of the courts, which used both religion and artistic expression as means of moral support as well as a justification of their power. Around the 5th-6th century AD, kingdoms and principalities of Indian influence had already taken shape in the southern part of Indochina, as well as in the Malaysian peninsula and beyond, in Sumatra and Java.

Archaeological finds seem to confirm that in the Malaysian peninsula and the southern delta regions of Burma (Myanmar), Thailand and Cambodia, both Hinduism and Buddhism made their appearance between the 1st and 3rd century AD, following the routes taken by traders and pilgrims that linked India and southern Burma, central-southern Siam, the delta zone of the Mekong River and the coastal strip of Vietnam. The rise and spread of the two great religions of India, together with the rich artistic and literary traditions of that country, not only brought the exportation of fascinating ceremonies and rituals, but also went hand in hand with the development of the first important state organizations in the region: commercial way stations or a part of federations of commercial way stations, which became political entities in order to defend themselves and to develop and coordinate their activities. Compared to the small Bronze Age kingdoms, these later ones had different origins and dimensions. Above all, they had a new identity.

25 - HARI-HARA (H. 45 IN.), A SYNCRETIC DIVINITY IN THE HINDU PANTHEON, TO WHOM THE KHMER DEDICATED A SPECIAL CULT (KIMBELL ART MUSEUM, FORT WORTH).

26 - A PATINATED BRONZE RECEPTACLE (H. 9.5 IN.), AN ARTIFACT OF THE DONG-SO'N CULTURE THAT CAN BE DATED TO THE 6TH-5TH CENTURY BC (MUSÉE GUIMET, PARIS).

27 - THIS DONG-SO'N BRONZE RITUAL DRUM (H. 24 IN., DIAMETER 30.7 IN.) FOUND IN VIETNAM, DATES TO THE 3RD-1ST CENTURY BC (MUSÉE GUIMET, PARIS).

For over a thousand years the influence of India managed to forge cultural unity among the various lands in the region. The Sanskrit and Pali languages, Indian writing, Theravada and Mahayana Buddhism, Brahmanic Hinduism (which is based on the Brahman, the union and synthesis of all individual souls—*atman*), and other currents of Hinduism all became widespread, both because of direct contact and through the diffusion of Indian mythological and philosophical literature, which had a particularly strong attraction for populations that for the most part were based on oral tradition but were quite receptive to

the introduction of writing systems modeled after those of India and who willingly enriched their languages with an "exalted" vocabulary mostly derived from India. The *Mahabharata* and *Ramayana* epics became especially popular and widespread, and proved to be an inexhaustible source of inspiration for the local literature and art.

The rulers of Funan and Chenla, the first state structures that left abundant traces in the contemporaneous and following civilizations, were Hindus. The proto-historic period is little documented except for legends and myths, but it was certainly marked by an improvement in the techniques employed in agriculture, animal husbandry, and ceramics in readily accessible localities that had privileged positions in broad river valleys or along the coasts. In any case, it was only in the first centuries of the Christian era that a civilization rose up as a true antecedent to that of Angkor.

28-29 - A DETAIL OF THE ROYAL PROCESSION, WHICH DERIVED FROM THE *RAMAYANA* EPIC, ON A STONE BAS-RELIEF IN THE NORTH PAVILION OF THE WEST GALLERY AT ANGKOR WAT.

29 - DETAIL OF THE BATTLE OF LANKA, ONE OF THE MAIN EPISODES IN THE *RAMAYANA*, SCULPTED IN BAS-RELIEF IN THE WEST GALLERY OF ANGKOR WAT.

# FUNAN AND CHENLA

The real name of this civilization is unknown, but 3rd-century AD Chinese chronicles refer to it as Funan, a probable distortion of the word *bnam* (*phnom,* in the modern Khmer language), which means "mountain." Despite its name, its sphere of influence was situated around the Mekong River delta and the southern coasts of present-day Cambodia and Vietnam. The population was probably of local origin and spoke a language that was part of the Mon-Khmer group. There is evidence that shows that Funan was a strong maritime state with a commercial bent. In the digs carried out at Oc Eo, in southern Vietnam, which was probably the most important city and river port in Funan, archaeologists found numerous artifacts that were the result of trade made with India, China and even the Roman Empire.

Little is known for certain about Funan except that it most likely had the power to ensure the safety of its trade routes and that it was governed efficiently. Many facets of its culture were certainly assimilated from India, the intermediaries being the Indian merchants, who were quite active at that time on the trade routes between the Arabian Peninsula and the Far East. It was they who most probably first introduced the cultural, philosophical and religious concepts that contributed to the development of this local kingdom. In fact, Indian influence proved to be essential even to the origin of the Funan civilization. While a local myth relates that the world was created by a king of the mythological serpents (*naga*) who supposedly drank the water that inundated the earth, thus causing the terra firma to emerge, historically this kingdom presumably originated from the marriage of an Indian Brahman, Kaundinya, and a local Nagas princess, Soma. Indeed, Brahmin influence must have been indispensable if it is true, as the Chinese

chronicles once again state, that exponents of the highest caste of Hinduism, the Brahmin, which safeguarded ancient Indian philosophical and religious knowledge, were encouraged to move to Funan to become counselors to various local rulers.

Nonetheless, despite the important influence of India, even concerning aspects outside religious practice such as politics, one cannot speak of the total 'Indianization' of the structures and population of Funan. In effect, this was partial Indianization, which was inherited by the successive states up to the Khmer empire.

Evidently, it was not only the pure, elevated religious and social-religious knowledge of India that sustained the growth and prestige of this kingdom suspended between history and legend, for this went hand in hand with a high-level knowledge of hydraulics and engineering. Aerial photographs taken during a research campaign in the 1930s revealed signs of extensive irrigation networks in various Funan sites. The capacity to channel the tumultuous waters of the Mekong in plots laid out expressly for agriculture implies that this kingdom was probably not only a maritime power, but that its survival was also based on efficient exploitation of the land. We know nothing for certain regarding the reasons behind the crisis suffered by Funan, when in the 6th century it was annexed to the kingdom of Chenla, which had formerly been its vassal and was probably another federation of city-states. This annexation was not particularly traumatic. In fact, the Funan population was gradually assimilated by the victorious people of Chenla. Chronologically, however, while Funan must have provided some of the basic elements of the Khmer civilization through osmosis, Chenla was on the other hand its direct predecessor.

According to Chinese documents, it seems that this kingdom was initially a vassal state of Funan, becoming independent around the year 550. And after about sixty years, again according to the chronicles of the Chinese Empire, Chenla managed to complete the annexation of its powerful rival and to absorb not only its population, but also most of its cultural values of Indian derivation. Unlike Funan, whose center lay outside the territory of present-day Cambodia, the first capital of Chenla was Ishanapura, which was founded around the year 613 near Sambor Prei Kuk, now in the Cambodian province of Kompong Thom. After annexing Funan, Chenla was divided into two parts, northern and southern, which Chinese historical sources refer to as "land Chenla" and "water Chenla." The heart of the northern section was the region of Champassak, in present-day Laos, while the southern one re-used the bor-

ders of Funan in the delta and the eastern coast. Around 715 AD, the two parts of Chenla underwent further fragmentation, which must have proved fatal for this kingdom. At that time—and this was probably the main cause of the weakening and division of Chenla as well as of Funan before then—the entire region was already feeling the pressure brought to bear by the expansion into parts of present-day southern Thailand and as far as the Strait of Malacca on the part of the Buddhist empire of Srivijaya, which from the island of Sumatra extended its sphere of influence over most of insular Asia. At the same time Sirvijaya ensured greater safety to its sea trade routes, which offered an opportunity for territorial, political and cultural expansion. It was this empire that dealt the death-blow to Chenla and laid the foundations for the rise of the Khmer empire. In that same period, parts of modern Burma and Thailand fell under the direct control or influence of the Mòn, another Buddhist population whose language was akin to that of the Khmer. Finally independent from Chenla dominion, but in turn unable to sustain the encounter with the powerful Javanese state, groups of the Khmer people withdrew from the coastal regions and moved further and further toward the interior, finally settling in the plains northwest of Tonlé Sap, the large lake in the middle of the hydrographic system of the middle-lower Mekong River, which is now the heart of present-day Cambodia. Here, under the leadership of an extraordinary personage, Jayavarman II, the foundations were laid for an empire destined to last for centuries.

# THE INDIAN INFLUENCE

From the 5th to the 13th century powerful states rose up in the region, characterized by architecture and figurative art strongly influenced by Buddhism. However, compared to the preceding Hinayana influence, this was not the result of long, fatiguing pilgrimages on the part of missionary monks or worshippers visiting the sacred sites of northern India. In this case the type of Buddhism was Mahayana, and it arrived directly from the Indian subcontinent via the sea routes that followed the regular monsoon seasons. This religious current, which evolved from the Doctrine of the Enlightened One, places emphasis on compassion and the common search for Illumination rather than on individual salvation and monastic life. The true stronghold of Hinduism from the 8th to the 13th century was Cambodia (and Java), whereas this religion never managed to become truly popular in Thailand, Burma, and Laos, where it was by no means a threat to the predominant Hinayana-Theravada Buddhism.

32 - HARI-HARA, PORTRAYED HERE IN A 7TH-CENTURY STONE HEAD IN LATERAL AND FRONTAL PERSPECTIVE (H. 17 IN.) FOUND AT PRASAT PHNOM DA, IS ONE OF THE DIVINITIES WHO COMBINES THE FEATURES OF SHIVA AND VISHNU (MUSÉE GUIMET, PARIS).

33 - THIS SANDSONE SCULPTURE OF VISHNU FOUND AT TUOL DAI BUON (H. 72 IN.) AND DATING FROM THE 6TH-7TH CENTURY, SHOWS THE FOUR HANDS OF THE GOD HOLDING A SPHERE, A CLUB, A SHELL AND A DISK OR WHEEL (NATIONAL MUSEUM, PHNOM PENH).

After Buddhism was almost uprooted in India as the result of the Islamic conquest of the subcontinent, during the 9th century the Mahayana current declined in Southeast Asia as well, being replaced by the Theravada doctrines, which were reintroduced by monks from Sri Lanka.

The iconography of Southeast Asian sculpture clearly reflects the Indian influences that began to penetrate the region in the Christian era and for the most part drew inspiration from religious sources. From an artistic standpoint, in all of Southeast Asia the personages of the Buddhist and Hindu pantheon were assimilated with original iconographic features, which were transmitted almost unaltered. However, the ideal of physical perfection and its rendering in sculpture produced different characteristics from those typical of India, such as the depiction of faces that stressed local physiognomy, or bodies with a detailed representation of the muscles and skeleton. Furthermore, the number of Hindu divinities worshipped in Southeast Asia was much smaller than in India. In fact, with few exceptions, they were reduced to the figures of Vishnu, Shiva, Ganesha and Hari-Hara (the combination of Vishnu and Shiva). In Buddhist sculpture the emphasis was placed on the exemplary role played by the bodhisattvas, especially Avalokiteshvara (the bodhisattva of compassion), as well as on the salvific function of Maitreya (the future Buddha).

The evolution of religious iconography in a local key began in Funan and Chenla. From an artistic standpoint, the stone sculptures produced in these two states—works that were so similar that at times one wonders whether the kingdoms were distinct and independent or were the same kingdom given different names by historical sources—achieve such perfection as to lead some scholars to assert that they may have been preceded by a more ancient tradition of wooden sculpture.

For centuries, dominion in southern Asia was disputed by the insular empire of Srivijaya to the south and the continental one of Pagan, which was based in Burma, to the north. Srivijaya in particular spread a sculpture style in the region that was strongly influenced by Mahayana Buddhism, as well as by Tantric Buddhism. The great number of statues of bodhisattvas (potential Buddhas worthy of Nirvana but who decide to remain in the world of the senses in order to help others attain enlightenment) which were produced in this period over a rather large area is a sign of an art that was still receptive to various influences while already mature, but it especially shows the strong attraction exerted by this religious current.

34 AND 35 - THREE EXAMPLES OF THE
HIGHLY REFINED PORTRAITURE IN THE PRE-
ANGKORIAN PERIOD. AT LEFT, A HEAD OF
BUDDHA DATING FROM THE 6TH-7TH
CENTURY (H. 11 IN.; NATIONAL MUSEUM,
PHNOM PENH). IN THE MIDDLE, THE WARRIOR
GOD SKANDA AND HIS MOUNT, A PEACOCK (H.
31.5 IN., L. 20 IN.), IN A SCULPTURE PIECE
FROM KDEI ANG (MUSÉE GUIMET, PARIS). AT
RIGHT, GANESHA, THE ELEPHANT-HEADED
GOD WHO WAS A PROMINENT FIGURE IN
KHMER SCULPTURE BEFORE THE FOUNDATION
OF ANGKOR, PORTRAYED HERE IN A 6TH-7TH-
CENTURY SANDSTONE STATUE (H. 29 IN.;
NATIONAL MUSEUM, PHNOM PENH).

36 - Maitreya, the bodhisattva often identified as the future Buddha, is one of the most common motifs in Khmer art. Here we see him in a 7th-8th-century sculpture (h. 11 in.; Musée Guimet, Paris).

37 - Curly hair, elongated ear lobes and arched eyebrows are the distinctive features of this head of Buddha (h. 8.5 in.), which was discovered in the Mekong River delta (Musée Guimet, Paris).

38 AND 39 LEFT - LOKESHVARA, THE BODHISATTVA OF COMPASSION AND CENTRAL FIGURE OF MAHAYANA BUDDHISM, IS PORTRAYED IN THIS HEAD (H 8.5 IN.) E AND FIGURE (AD 650-700, H. 31.5 IN.) (MUSÉE GUIMET, PARIS).

39 RIGHT - MAITREYA, THE BUDDHA WHO IS STILL TO COME, WITH HIS HANDS IN FOUR DIFFERENT *MUDRA* POSITIONS (H. 18 IN.; MUSÉE GUIMET, PARIS).

## THE ORIGINS OF THE KHMER

This was the geographic, political, religious and cultural context in which the history of the Khmer began. Many aspects of this population are still wrapped in mystery, beginning with its origin. The Khmer were probably part of the Paleo-Indonesian ethnic group, and in the 2nd century BC their presence is documented in Indochina, in the "pre-delta" region of the Mekong (Bassac, now in Vietnam). Up to the 6th century AD, as Chinese sources inform us, they were vassals of Funan. Once this latter man I, who commissioned the Prei Khmeng. From the end of the 7th century to the beginning of the 9th century, only the stones—used to build the Prasat Andet, Prasat Ak Yum and Kompong Preah—bear witness to the consolidation of Khmer power, which by then had become independent, while historical sources tell us little indeed about the customs of the population and the political situation in this region. After another obscure period, in the 9th century Jayavarman II, who probably hailed from Srivijaya,

state disintegrated, a Khmer group known as *Kambuja* ("children of Kambu"–a figure in Hindu mythology) founded an independent kingdom north of Tonlé Sap. Historic sources transmit nothing more than the echoes of this chaotic period, called pre-Angkor. This obscure phase must have ended only in the early 9th century with the emergence of the names of the rulers who literally began to lay the foundation stones of the Khmer empire: Bhavavarman I, who is associated with construction of Phnom Da; Isanavarman I, the builder of Sambor Prei Kuk; and Jayavar-the island kingdom to which the Khmer were to some degree subject and where his family had presumably been forced into exile because of the circumstances in Indochina, unified the country and founded four cities in the area where Angkor later rose up. His descendants extended Khmer dominion toward Laos to the north, Siam to the west, taking in the Mekong Delta to the south, and to the east as far as the Red River; in northern Vietnam, when they defeated the powerful Champa kingdom and thus found themselves facing the southern China Sea.

40-41 - On a sandstone lintel from Kompong Thom (h. 21.5 in., l. 73 in.), the king and his court are depicted under the protection of a bodhisattva (National Museum, Phnom Penh).

42 TOP - THE PRIMARY CHARACTERISTIC OF THE MONUMENTS OF SAMBOR PREI KUK IS THAT THEY WERE MADE OF BRICK, WHILE STONE WAS USED ONLY FOR THE DECORATIVE ELEMENTS, A FEATURE OF THE EARLIEST ARCHITECTURE AT ANGKOR.

42 BOTTOM - A BATTLE BETWEEN SOME MEN AND A LION. FROM AN ARCHITECTURAL AND SCULPTURAL STANDPOINT, SAMBOR PREI KUK ANTICIPATES MANY ELEMENTS OF THE FUTURE ANGKORIAN CIVILIZATION.

43 - A CLASSIC HORSESHOE ARCH, OR *KUDU*, OF INDIAN DERIVATION, DECORATES THE SIDE OF A CELLA MADE OF SANDSTONE BLOCKS AT SAMBOR PREI KUK. THIS TYPE OF DECORATION IMITATES TRADITIONAL WOODEN ARCHITECTURE.

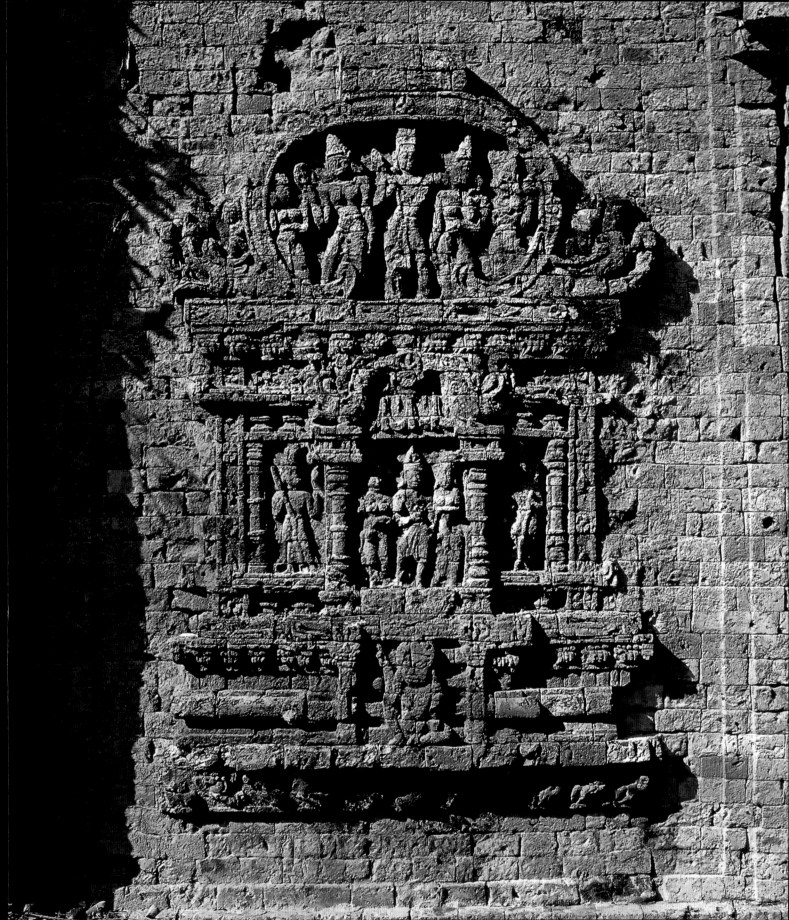

# 2

# THE DAWN
# OF THE EMPIRE

# THE ROOTS OF A CIVILIZATION

Whether it was the heir of ancient confederations such as Funan and Chenla (whose very existence has been called into question by scholars such as Claude Jacques on the basis of the translation of epigraphs in the Khmer language, sources that for a long time were underestimated with respect to the inscriptions carved in Sanskrit and, even more, with respect to later Chinese sources) or, —in a more direct manner, the result of the internal evolution of the Khmer— the Angkor empire, under the influence of Mahayana Buddhism but with strong Hindu features, dominated most of continental Southeast Asia, over which it constructed impressive architectural works, between the 9th and 13th century AD. Indeed, it has been calculated that about 900 temples alone were built in Cambodia and Thailand. Angkor, with a religious and civic complex that at its height was able to house and support one million inhabitants, was the center of this architectural development. And although some scholars— such as Australian archaeologist and expert in pre-industrial urban civilizations Roland Fletcher— believe that it has not been proven that Angkor was a city that was really inhabited, the large temple cities of the region (built for the most part near present-day Siem Reap) are the immortal testimony of the successors of Jayavarman II, the founder of the Khmer empire, and the pride of a nation in the following centuries, so much so that to this day the profile of Angkor Wat stands out on the flag of the Democratic Republic of Cambodia. However, like all great civilizations, the Khmer also had a history that was not always linear and went through alternating periods of development and decline most probably due to causes that were both human and environmental. And like all great civilizations, the overall image projected by its material remains and, indirectly, through the accounts of contemporaneous and posthumous sources, is that of its most prosperous, most creative and influential age, which for the sake of convenience we could call "classic."

The classic Khmer period lies between the years 802 and 1327, that is, between the ascension to the throne of Jayavarman II and the death of Shrindrajayavarman. This age contains all the salient features of the Khmer civilization, without excluding the pre-existence or persistence of some of them in this long passage of time: a universal monarch at the head of a state with imperial characteristics; a capital, Angkor, that was almost unique in the period of time under discussion; Hinduism and Mahayana Buddhism as the state religion; religious architecture mostly of stone (sandstone or laterite) and with some wood; state temples also used for the cult of the dynasty; worship of the creative power inherent in the cosmos, which is identified with the *linga*, the stone symbol of Shiva's phallus, that is, of the creative power of the cosmos; tower sanctuaries (*prasats*) that house the images of the gods, often with a quincunx layout and supported by terraced pyramids; important and extensive hydraulic works, including canal networks and huge artificial reservoirs (*barays*); a network of large roads, rest stations, and brick bridges; inscriptions in Khmer or Sanskrit (the last one is dated precisely 1327); iconography that is mostly Hindu, deriving in particular from the Indian epic poems and from the *Purana*.

Up to the year 802 the configuration of Khmer politics consisted of numerous kingdoms based on the clan system, whose homogeneous ethnic and cultural makeup did not manage to avoid a state of permanent conflict, either between the clans themselves or with neighboring powers such as the Cham, who lived in present-day central Vietnam. The ascension to the throne of Jayavarman I in 657 can be considered the beginning of what is known as the Angkorian period of Khmer civilization. Not all scholars agree that this ruler was the first Khmer emperor. But the fact remains that during his reign Khmer power was consolidated in the territories wrested from Funan.

It is significant that since this king had no male heirs, for more than a century after his death in 681 the fragile kingdom was subject to fragmentation and anarchy, and even risked extinction. At the end of the 8th century the crisis of Chenla, which had inherited the territory and cultural features of Funan, led to the extension of the Javanese protectorate over this region and its population, including the semi-independent Khmer groups. Yet the time was perhaps ripe for change, which had been made necessary by a situation in which strong and extensive political powers emerged, founded on more evolved cultures and on religious beliefs that had the mark of universality. A catalyst was needed, and this was a figure who was both great and mysterious: Jayavarman II. This is the name used in various chronicles and inscriptions and by which he universally known. However, the posthumous title ascribed to him by his descendants is Parameshvara ("Supreme Lord"), an appellation that raises him to both a mythological and political level, positions that were inseparable from the Khmer concept and definition of power.

At this stage, however, we must go back in time a bit in order to understand the context in which the events of Jayavarman II's rule took place. The fortune of the Khmer of Angkor began with the disintegration of Chenla and with the resultant possibility offered to the enterprising leaders of Khmer stock to lay claim to land and power. The Khmer epic, the tale of a people divided and of uncertain pedigree who achieved glory as one of the greatest Asiatic empires for five centuries, has been reconstructed by means of their monuments and relief sculpture, the artifacts found during archaeological digs, and the inscriptions carved in Pali, Sanskrit and Khmer that were found within the confines of the ancient empire. The inscriptions provide us with genealogies and chronologies that help to reconstruct an outline of this civilization, as well as a heterogeneous mass of data that range from the virtues of the individual sovereigns to the details regarding the foundation, architects and patrons of the temples and the political-administrative organization of the empire. It is this great amount of information concerning the official, political and religious sphere that leaves great gaps in our knowledge of daily life, not only of the common people but also of the nobles and military men, almost as if only the supernatural—and however much of it was contemplated in everyday life and in politics and religion—was truly important or worthy of being mentioned. This was so true that even such a major figure in Khmer history as Jayavarman II was—except for secondary sources—left in the background. So far no inscription found dates directly to his reign, and the main source of information we have on him is the stele of Sdok Kak Thom, which was carved two centuries after his death. This stele, which was found in southeastern Thailand, was dedicated to the *purohita* (the leading officiant of Hindu tradition) of the court of Udayadityavarman II (11th century), tells us that Jayavarman was a guest of the Javanese Sailendra dynasty and later returned to Cambodia. The reason for this stay and its duration are still vague. Arab sources speak of a naval expedition on the part of the Sailendra that arrived at the capital of the Khmer kingdom, which had settled along the banks of the Tonlé Sap. After killing the young Khmer king and having made his kingdom their vassal, the expedition withdrew, taking with it some hostages, including the future king. The chronicles that make more direct references to Jayavarman do not mention his stay on the island of Java, and this leads one to believe that he really came from the Malaysian peninsula or from another territory under the dominion of the Sailendra Empire.

## UNDER THE SHADOW OF THE GOD-KING

The date of the future emperor's return from Indonesia, or from a land that in any case was under Javanese dominion, is uncertain, but was most probably around 790. Afterward, for twelve years he engaged in skillful military campaigns to reinforce his power and expand the territory under his control, which for the most part consisted of small Khmer principalities scattered along the course of the Mekong River. During this period Jayavarman also looked for a safe and stable site for his capital city. After some time spent traveling about and founding temporary cities, the birth of his first stable capital, Indrapura, on the lower course of the great Indochinese river, was a sign of his having consolidated his power. But evidently this was not enough, because he again moved his power center to various other localities, until he finally decided on the definitive site of Hariharalaya, near future Angkor, in what is now the area of Roluos, on the broad irrigated plain north of the Tonlé Sap ("Great Lake"), which has the same name as its effluent. The reason behind these frequent moves was probably the ruler's search for a site with the best potential for food supply as well as for defense. In any case, all the capitals were founded in pre-existing ancient cities, a choice that was probably partly due to the need to sever all ties with Java or with a continental territory under Javanese dominion to some extent. Be that as it may, Jayavarman's choice was felicitous for various motives, not the last of which was the possibility to control the flow of much of the region's water resources.

In 802, on Phnom Kulen (*Mahendraparvata*, the "Mountain of the Great Indra"), there was a solemn ceremony officiated by influential Brahmins to crown Jayavarman for the second time with the title *Hindu* of *Chakravartin* ("Lord of the Wheel", or "Emperor of the World"), and to commemorate this event a temple to Shiva was constructed. This ceremony must have been the foundation stone of the Khmer civilization and one of the epoch-making moments in the history of Indochina. At the same time, however, it was an eminently political event, with an innovative feature. Jayavarman had himself proclaimed ruler of all the Khmer with a ritual borrowed from Hinduism that would make him a *Devaraja*, or god-king, thus elevating Shiva–a favorite divinity in the Khmer religious sphere for a long time–to the rank of guardian of the dynasty and the empire. Having thus established himself as the terrestrial counterpart of the god, Jayavarman II proclaimed his absolute authority and sovereignty and the definitive rupture with Java. Thus, from the outset the concept of the emperor's divine nature and the assimilation of a great many Indian and Hindu elements lay at the base of a political strategy aimed at providing motivation and a solid basis for a common Khmer civilization, while at the same time guaranteeing the people's absolute respect of their sovereign. In the last analysis this move guaranteed the future of a strong empire and great civilization. And the very choice of the region in which the first capital, Hariharalaya, was founded (dedicated to Hari-Hara, a divinity who combines the features of Shiva and Vishnu) and the successive construction of the temple complex of Mahendraparvata (up to the return to Hariharalaya a short time before Jayavarman's death) was by no means casual, as it complied with a precise strategy. The principal enemies of the new state were in fact located to the south and east, and it would have been very difficult to reach and attack the heart of the Khmer kingdom, which lay in a remote area in the midst of thick forests and was accessible only by way of as unpredictable a waterway as the Tonlé Sap. This was a successful strategy indeed, since the Khmer lost only one naval battle–against the Cham in 1177–in six centuries. After founding his empire, Jayavarman (*Jaya*=victorious, and *Varman*=shield, protector) initiated a series of military campaigns to extend his territory and at the same time make it safer. During his rule the regions of Chenla were united and given the dynastic name of Kambuja, that is, "Land of the Children of Kambu", an ascetic in Hindu mythology.

48 - This *makara* in the Phnom Kulen style decorated a lintel (h. 99 in., l. 31,5 in.) in the temple of Prasat Koki (Musée Guimet, Paris).

49 - The temple of Prasat Koki houses the image of a king (h. 99 in.) and two servants. This representation identifies the monarch with the bodhisattva (Musée Guimet, Paris).

## SOCIETY AND RELIGION

Ancient Khmer society revolved around the figure of the king, who was considered a god, and was structured into classes: the royal oligarchy, the priests, the army, the civil population—organized in handicrafts guilds, commerce being managed by the women and Chinese—and the slaves. The decisive role played by religion in the Khmer social-political context is revealed by the fact that the leading priests were of Indian descent and transmitted their posts in matrilinear succession, a fact that, together with the others, reveals the close contact between the Khmer and Indian civilizations and the probable presence of several basic ancient elements in common.

In the first centuries of the Christian era there was a strong but pacific "Indianization" of Indochina on the part of the Brahmins, the Hindu priestly caste and, at a later stage, by Bud-

50, 51, 52-53 and 54-55 - Officers riding elephants, foreign warriors (perhaps allies or Chinese mercenaries), and combat elephants transporting the king or members of his family (who can be identified by their parasols, which were a symbol of royalty) file past the observer in the outstanding series of bas-relief panels that decorate the East Gallery of the Bayon (12th-13th century). The subject in this case is mostly military, as opposed to the civil or religious scenes in the inner galleries.

dhist missionaries. The Brahmins brought the great Indian culture to Cambodia at the request of the local political elites themselves, who viewed the complex Hindu ritual as a means of consecrating their recently acquired dominion. Later on, and in some areas contemporaneously, the Buddhist monks spread the original message of Buddha among the population, and were followed a few centuries later by emissaries of a new form of Buddhism, Mahayana. By taking root in a substratum that was at once Hindu, Buddhist and animistic, this religion ended up replacing Hinduism as the official state religion (but did not manage to undermine the power of the priesthood), and to this day 88% of the population follows Mahayana practices.

56-57 - The king administering justice stands out among the high-quality relief sculpture in the Bayon.

58 - EXTRAORDINARY SCENES OF
DAILY LIFE (TOP) ANIMATE THE
LOWER BAND OF THE OUTER
SOUTH GALLERY OF THE BAYON,
WHOSE MAIN THEME, HOWEVER, IS
THE NAVAL BATTLE OF TONLÉ
SAP, WHICH THE KHMER WON IN
1181 AGAINST THE CHAM:

BOTTOM, A CHAM WARRIOR IS
DEPICTED ON A SHIP IN HIS FLEET.

58-59 - A CART LIKE THOSE
STILL USED IN CAMBODIA
FOLLOWS THE MILITARY PARADE IN
THE EAST GALLERY OF THE
BAYON.

Over the centuries and during the period of its diffusion, the term "Hinduism" has indicated a specific religious tradition of Indian derivation, but it is in itself extraneous to the tradition of its land of origin. Besides its foreign derivation, which is Persian to be precise, it is applied as if it were a unique religious experience to a context that rejects any definition of the religious phenomenon that is too restrictive, preferring to identify it in its multiple nature as a series of paths toward liberation. In fact, Hinduism now stands for a set of practices that originated sometime between the II and I Millennium BC but

matured over a period of several centuries. These practices are the result of the encounter on Indian soil between groups of Indo-European stock—in particular their religious and cultural ideas, which were similar to those of the ancient Greeks and Romans—and local religious, cultural and social elements. There are three basic sources: the Veda, traditionally viewed as elaborations of the intuitions or visions of officiants and hermits who lived in the forests; the mythological texts (including the Ramayana and Mahabharata sagas); and a set of sacred texts of various origin and contents that clarify and interpret the preceding texts in the light of concrete application and later experiences: the Agama, Shastra, and Sutras, as well as the Pu-

rana, ancient stories concerning legendary personages. All of these texts were written in Sanskrit, although there are also later analyses and translations written in the middle and modern Indian language. The knowledge and transmission of Sanskrit, which is indispensable for the performance of the rituals, is one of the prerogatives of the priests or Brahmans, who are therefore at the apex of a system that originally also included warriors and rulers (Khatriya), farmers, artisans and merchants (Vaisya), and servants, peasants and laborers (Shudra) but that now embraces something like 3,000 castes and sub-castes of a religious, professional and ethnic nature. In India, at the base of the caste pyramid are the dalit (the "excluded," a word that has now replaced the much abused terms "untouchable" and "pariah" or Gandhi's over-optimistic term harijan, "sons of God"), the animistic and tribal minorities, and foreigners. While it is primarily through respect of the caste rules, with its gamut of benefits and discrimination, that the individual obtains by birth his/her role in society and, above all, can aspire to liberation, this path to liberation, which we could call legalist and which originated in the Veda, is flanked by two others. One is devotional and is rooted in mythology, its greatest expression lying in the cult of Vishnu (the preserver) and especially in his reincarnation Krishna, as manifestations of a single supreme divinity. The other path is ascetic and harks back to parts of the Veda (such as the Upanishad) as well as to a parallel tradition with a strong local influence that, following the example of Shiva (the destroyer), promotes a personal quest for salvation in impenetrable places through psycho-physical techniques that favor the revelation of the ultimate and transcendent reality. The cult of Brahma, the third element (that of the creator) in the Trimurti, is now quite limited in India because its abstract dimension was not very congenial to the religious evolution of this country. The fact that each of these divinities, like others in the immense Hindu pantheon, is connected to an entire series of symbols, objects, female counterparts, and mounts, explains the proliferation of iconography of religious inspiration, which partly migrated by way of the trade routes and conquests in most of South and Southeast Asia, where it was modified while maintaining its true meaning and spirit.

60 - SHIVA, REPRESENTED HERE (CENTER) SURROUNDED BY HIS DISCIPLES ON THE SOUTH GALLERY OF THE BAYON, COMPETED WITH VISHNU AS THE MOST POPULAR GOD AMONG THE ANCIENT KHMER OF HINDU FAITH.

61 - THE KHMER HAD ONLY A MINOR CULT DEDICATED TO BRAHMA, A DIVINITY THAT IS REPRESENTED RATHER INFREQUENTLY. THIS SCULPTURE (H. 43 IN.) DATES FROM THE MID-19TH CENTURY.

Buddhism was born during the time of the philosophical speculation centered around the *Upanishad*, in the 6th century BC–a fervent period marked by religious activity and the quest for the Truth that gave rise to Jainism in India, Zoroastrianism in Iran and Taoism in China–and from the outset was characterized by its rigorous doctrine and at the same time its universalism.

The basic concept elaborated by Buddha and handed down to his original followers is quite simple: existence is suffering that is caused by craving and attachment. By eliminating this desire and grasping the ultimate reality hidden behind sensory illusions and the distortions of mental impressions, one can achieve liberation from death and suffering and attain nirvana, which means liberation or, more literally, cessation and extinction.

In India the very first images of Buddha were created centuries after his death, thus overriding (partly thanks to the influence of Hinduism) the original Buddhist aversion for all types of human images, in particular of Buddha.

Parallel to the evolution of a Buddhist iconography that gradually embraced influences from Iran, Central Asia, South Asia and the Far East, there was the development of common elements that served to individualize Buddha (and, in a later stage, the bodhisattvas) among the host of different images that were often associated with ascetics as well as with princes or divine or semi-divine beings of other religious traditions. Thus, 32 special distinguishing marks were included in the representation, which more often that not was stereotyped. Obviously, it was not possible to include all these features in a single image, but at least one or more of them had to be part of the portrait. And this was precisely what often distinguished one image of Buddha from another. One of the most important and most utilized of these was the *ushnisha*, a sort of chignon on the top of his head symbolizing the wisdom of Buddha; others were his elongated ear lobes (a sign of nobility) and the dot between his eyes (a sign of clairvoyance). The Buddha's entire body was depicted in a stylized manner and rarely included anatomical details, unless they helped to express the particular character of that portrait (for example, ascetic tension, or renunciation, or again, the power of doctrine against evil). The stereotypical nature of Buddhist sculpture, which naturally had its exceptions, hardly prevailed because of the ancient sculptors' incapacity to reproduce the human body with precision. On the contrary, the Khmer artisans and artists probably went through long, meticulous training that allowed them, after years of experience, to carve, with confidence and skill and on more and more precious stone, the traditional and devotional images as well as satisfy the motives and taste of their patrons. A difficult task indeed. For this reason, and because of the significance and value attached to continuity in Asia, especially in a civilization devoted to immortality, the repetition and apparent indifference to all innovation in the sculpture was transformed into a standard established to represent to the utmost the features called for in a particular image in order to express the superiority of Buddha, his spirituality, and his universal compassion. In Khmer art, in which the image of Buddha was soon replaced by that of the bodhisattvas and was then revived under the Thai and Theravada Buddhist influence, at the heart of the Mahayana doctrine, the body is often sexless in order to underscore the Buddha's capacity to dominate craving. The legs are crossed in the lotus position, and the hands determine the disposition of the specific image (protection, meditation, teaching, etc.). The Buddha's eyes are usually half-closed in the shape of lotus buds and his mouth has a barely perceptible smile, the subtle smile of one who has achieved the ultimate liberation.

62 - BRONZE STATUE OF BUDDHA (H. 36 IN.) SEATED ON THE *NAGA* MUCHILINDA, WHO IS PROTECTING HIM. THIS FIND CAME FROM BINH DIH, IN VIETNAM AND DATES FROM THE LATE 12TH CENTURY (NATIONAL MUSEUM, PHNOM PENH).

63 LEFT - AN ELABORATE BRONZE PORTRAIT OF BUDDHA BEING PROTECTED BY A SEVEN-HEADED *NAGA* (H. 19.5 IN.). THIS STATUE

WAS SCULPTED IN THE LATE 12TH-EARLY 13TH CENTURY (NATIONAL MUSEUM, PHNOM PENH).

63 CENTER AND RIGHT - THE TWO DECORATED SIDES OF A *CAITYA* (H. 90.5 IN.) —A BUDDHIST MONUMENT USED TO HOUSE THE ASHES OF ILLUSTRIOUS PERSONS—WERE EXECUTED AT THE END OF THE 10TH CENTURY (MUSÉE GUIMET, PARIS).

The death of such a great figure as Jayavarman II, which occurred in 850, could not but trigger a dynastic crisis, which continued for several years. Khmer inscriptions furnish us with the names of no fewer than 39 Khmer monarchs in the Angkor period who were called upon to rule, not always because of lineage but, on the contrary, very often in the wake of turbulent events that marked moments of crisis for the empire. This did not depend exclusively on the armed pressure brought to bear by neighboring powers or by the capacity to deal with floods and famine in an efficacious manner. Part of the responsibility lay with the basic clan structure of the Khmer aristocracy.

When a king died, the person who at a certain time was at the apex of the clan hierarchy automatically had the right the ascend the throne, but his role was subject to the demands of prestigious exponents of the various branches of the clan, demands based on the fact that the lineage could be either patrilineal or matrilineal, with the added factor of the frequent practice of polygamy; hence the multiplication of pretenders to the throne, and the fractionalization of the clan and the clan's territory into cadet branches.

However, it seems that after the brief interregnum and crisis, the reign of Jayavarman III (854-877), the son of Jayavarman

II, was marked by peace and stability, and this may perhaps explain the scanty information we have regarding this ruler. We know that he began the construction of the sacred edifices of Hariharalaya, and the Prasat Kok Po and the Prasat Prei Monti in particular, in the vigorous archaic Phnom Kulen style, are attributed to him. His posthumous name, Vishnuloka, refers to his preference for Vishnu, the god with the universal character who, by means of his attributes and those of his divine descents to the Earth (avatara), which are scarcely represented in Khmer Hindu art, embraces in fact the entire gamut of human experiences that are interpreted and managed by the king, who is linked to the god. The Prasat Kok Po still has two brick towers in the middle of a complex surrounded by a moat, and on the surviving lintels there are images of Vishnu and his mount, the vulture Garuda. The three brick towers at Prei Monti, only parts of which are still standing, rise up over a carpet of leaves and moss. Among the few reliefs that are still legible, an outstanding one depicts Indra, an Indo-European thunderbolt divinity and king of the gods, carved on a lintel. This was the appropriate time to provide an empire that was now vast and temporarily pacified with a site worthy of such grandeur and, perhaps even more, of the aspirations of its rulers.

64 AND 65 - AN ELEMENT FROM A LINTEL AT THE PRASAT KOK PO (H. 31.5 IN., L. 95 IN.), IN WHICH THE VULTURE GARUDA IS THE MOUNT OF THE GOD VISHNU, WHO IS DEPICTED HERE RIDING ON HIS SHOULDERS. ON EITHER SIDE OF THE GOD, THE TERRIFYING KALA DEMONS ARE HOLDING TWO NAGA SERPENTS (MUSÉE GUIMET, PARIS).

From 877 to 889, Indravarman I (whose dynastic name was Isvaraloka), probably the grandson of one of Jayavarman II's wives and certainly one of the other great Khmer rulers, enlarged the small capital city of Hariharalaya and began building a temple city at Angkor, together with the construction of a network of canals and large reservoirs to control the flow of the water. His works, more than that of other kings, brought the Angkor civilization closer to the concept of hydraulic civilization as defined by several scholars, which links the management of water—both for productive and ritual purposes—to the emperor's function and prerogative of coordination and absolute control. This concept has been hotly debated but, without ignoring a series of other recently acquired elements connected to the daily life and administration of the empire and to the figure of the king, it at least provides us with a precise reference to Angkor civilization.

The small site of Hariharalaya (now know as the Roluos Group) was almost entirely a creation of Indravarman I, and its urban layout and architecture served as a model for the entire classical period. This ruler is also to be credited with creating the vast *baray* called Indratataka ("Indra's Sea") in the capital. This prodigious work was begun only five days after Indravarman's coronation; the immense rectangular reservoir, 12,500 feet long and 2,600 feet wide, could contain up to 24,600,000 cubic feet of water, much of which was used as the city's water supply and to irrigate the surrounding land. Furthermore, Bakgong Indravarman I also inaugurated the tradition of the huge state temples or temple mountains, and made do with the more modest but elegant Preah Ko dynastic temple to commemorate his ancestors. These two elements, the large reservoir and temple mountain (which almost every king would place beside his dynastic temple), would become the fundamental means by which all future Khmer sovereigns would display their grandeur. It is highly likely that the wooden palace of Indravarman was located inside the Preah Ko enclosure. Bakong, on the other hand, stood to the south of the latter. This terraced pyramid, which was used for the cult of Shiva and surrounded by a double wall, is the obvious precursor of Angkor Wat and Angkor Thom. Symbolically it is the representation of Mt. Meru, the home of the gods according to Hindu mythology. The large central tower is dressed with sandstone from Phnom Kulen, while the eight towers surrounding it are made of bricks and have stucco decoration. The end of the "central Meru," made of stone, is probably a reconstruction done in a later period which, like the original, presumably housed the *linga*, the phallic image of Shiva. The main entrance of this complex lies to the east, the direction considered holy because it reminds us of the divine nature of the king crowned by the gods who live in the East. Probably once crowded with minor religious buildings, Bakong now houses a community of Theravada monks, thus guaranteeing the ongoing operation of a school and various cult edifices.

66

66 LEFT - ONE OF THE EIGHT SANCTUARY TOWERS THAT SURROUND THE CENTRAL AREA OF BAKONG: THE DECORATION IS VERY ELEGANT, ESPECIALLY ON THE FALSE DOORS.

66 RIGHT - THE SHIVAITE COMPLEX OF BAKONG, WHICH WAS BUILT AT THE END OF THE 9TH CENTURY BY INDRAVARMAN I, WAS PROBABLY THE FIRST TEMPLE-MOUNTAIN IN THE ANGKOR AREA.

67 - THIS DETAIL OF THE SURVIVING DECORATION ON THE SOUTH WALL OF THE FIFTH TIER OF THE BAKONG DEMONSTRATES THE SKILL OF THE KHMER ARTISANS, WHICH WAS TESTED TO THE FULLEST IN THESE TEMPLE-MOUNTAINS.

Preah Ko ("Sacred Bull") was named after the image of Shiva's mount, the bull Nandin, which lies in the enclosure. Consecrated to this god in 880 and set on a laterite platform, Preah Ko was dedicated to Indravarman I's parents, to his maternal ancestors, to the founder of the dynasty, Jayavarman II, and his wife. All these persons were represented by statues, in various poses and of varying size, of Shiva and his consort. With its six towers and the structures made of alternating bricks and stone, Preah Ko is an extremely interesting monument. However, it must be said that it is known most of all for the sculpted figures of guardians (dvarapala) and female divinities (devata), as well as for the elegance of its sandstone lintels, their supports, and the false doors that decorate the towers. From this beautified and enlarged capital Indravarman I extended Khmer dominion to the west, as far as the Khorat plateau in Thailand. The prosperity of the kingdom, together with the period of peace, allowed this ruler to utilize the nation's commercial and agricultural resources in grand projects. The complicated network of dikes and canals built during the reign of Indravarman I and his successors was in fact the key to the prosperity that Angkor enjoyed for five centuries; in fact, it meant that the farmers no longer had to depend on the monsoons for their water supply and could produce more than enough rice for the population.

When Indravarman I died in 889, the Khmer state had already consolidated its territorial, ideological and cultural bases. Furthermore, it had solid stone foundations on which it would erect its myth in future centuries. However, it is no easy task to ascertain the boundaries of the Khmer empire, which once again are defined by the accounts carved on the steles and the invocations of the king's name found in sites in eastern Thailand. The many epithets commemorating the king ("a lion among the kings", "the prince who possesses all virtues", etc.) revive the image of a great sovereign at the head of a state that was at once strong militarily and respected for the justice that prevailed therein.

A serious dynastic crisis between the two direct successors broke out upon the death of Indravarman I. This conflict, which according to some historians even included naval battles on the Tonlé Sap lake, ended with the victory of Yasovardana, who during his coronation in 890 assumed the throne name of Yasovarman ("Protected by Glory").

68 TOP LEFT - THE FALSE ENTRANCE TO ONE OF THE CENTRAL TOWERS OF THE PREAH KO COMPLEX HAS STONE ELEMENTS INSERTED INTO THE BRICK STRUCTURE.

68 BOTTOM LEFT - ONE OF THE CENTRAL TOWERS OF THE PREAH KO (THE SO-CALLED SACRED BULL). THIS TEMPLE, LIKE THE BAKONG, IS PART OF THE ROLUOS GROUP AT ANGKOR AND, LIKE THE LATTER TEMPLE, IS MADE OF BRICKS.

68 RIGHT - ONCE COVERED WITH STUCCOWORK DECORATION, THE SIX CENTRAL TOWERS OF THE PREAH KO STAND OUT FOR THEIR ELEGANT BAS-RELIEF SCULPTURE, FINELY WROUGHT LINTELS, FALSE DOORS AND COLUMNS.

69 - A GARUDA, PART OF THE DECORATION ON THE CENTRAL TOWERS OF PREAH KO, IS HOLDING TWO NAGAS, HIS TRADITIONAL ENEMIES, BY THE TAIL.

# THE EMPIRE OF STONE

It was the Hindu architectural and decorative tradition more than the Buddhist one that inspired the great temples in the Cambodian jungle that bear witness to a unique and fascinating combination of local and imported elements. In the works that are often immense, as well as in the more modest but highly elegant temples or sanctuaries, the Khmer ancestor cult, and those revolving around sacred sites, assimilated the Hindu ideal of the *chakravartin*, or universal monarch, the lord of social order and guardian of the eternal law, and the myths of the cosmic mountain, the axis of the world.

All this was sanctioned for the first time in the 9th century through a grandiose Brahman ritual celebrated on Phnom Kulen for King Jayavarman II, who received, as a pledge of his alliance with the god Shiva, the *linga*, the phallic stone that symbolizes the god and which from that moment also became a visible testimony of his power (with the rise of Buddhism the *linga* was replaced by the image of Buddha). Thus was born the myth of the *devaraja*, the god-king, protector of the universe, whose abode could be nothing other than the temple mountain. Therefore, each king erected a personal temple during his reign that housed the *linga*, the symbol of his regality and his divine essence. Upon his death the temple became his mausoleum as well as a sort of architectural body: the most powerful kings or emperors built dynastic temples that not only expressed the hope for eternal life but also became a type of bridge between their ancestors

and their successors. All Khmer architecture was inspired by the symbolism of the cosmic mountain, the place where the world of men and the world of the gods communicated and in effect interacted, and it was precisely the square sanctuary tower with a terraced pyramid that was the most ancient Khmer architectural creation, made of brick, sandstone or laterite. At first isolated and later placed together on a platform in groups of three or five, the towers evolved into the theatrical complex of the quincunx temple mountain, four at the corners of the square perimeter and one in the middle, all connected by columned galleries. Nothing was left to chance or to the whims of patrons and architects. It was the myths concerning the origin of the world, which came from distant India, that imposed the rules of construction. The temple mountain was to stand, if possible, by a reservoir symbolizing the primordial ocean, whose chaotic depths contain life waiting to be manifested by a work: the Churning of the Ocean of Milk, which lies at the heart of the primary Hindu myths, which were promptly assimilated by the Khmer, a population that was indissolubly linked with water. The importance of the *baray*, the large Khmer artificial reservoir, played a fundamental role in the construction of the religious centers. Royal power was based not only on its sacred motivations, but also on the ruler's capacity to harness and exploit the water to irrigate the rice paddies, thus placing myth in a practical dimension and becoming the dispenser of life.

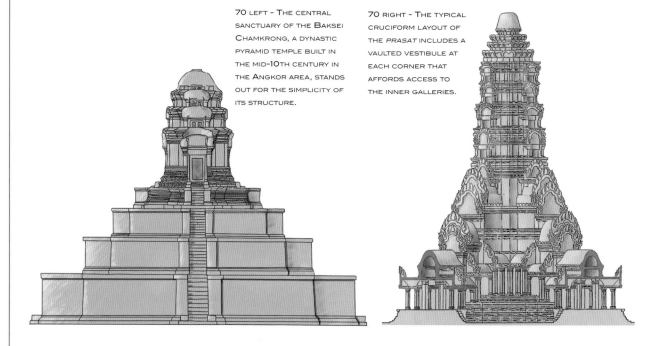

70 LEFT - THE CENTRAL SANCTUARY OF THE BAKSEI CHAMKRONG, A DYNASTIC PYRAMID TEMPLE BUILT IN THE MID-10TH CENTURY IN THE ANGKOR AREA, STANDS OUT FOR THE SIMPLICITY OF ITS STRUCTURE.

70 RIGHT - THE TYPICAL CRUCIFORM LAYOUT OF THE *PRASAT* INCLUDES A VAULTED VESTIBULE AT EACH CORNER THAT AFFORDS ACCESS TO THE INNER GALLERIES.

The main body of the temple stands for the mythical Mt. Meru, which in Indian religion is the center of the universe and symbolizes the regulative axis that transforms the original chaos into the manifest world. The five peaks of Mt. Meru are mirrored in the five symmetrically placed towers of the temple.

The protuberant gates on the special pavilions at the four cardinal points outside the structure celebrate the extension of royal power to embrace the entire universe. The bridge with the balustrade made up of serpents connects the residential areas and the temple—that is, the world of humans and that of the gods— and refers to the rainbow that links the sky and earth and, in the obsessive presence of the *naga*, to the rain brought by the serpents.

For that matter, every element in the structure has a mythological, allegorical or multiple meaning and serves to emphasize the divine dimension of edifices that are actual symbolic microcosms: the swans and the *garuda*, the mythical creatures usually recognizable as large birds of prey, which appear at the base of the constructions, tell us that these latter are nothing more or less than chariots of the gods in the form of flying palaces. In the interior, the presence of the statues in the guise of Shiva, Vishnu or bodhisattvas underscores the elevation of the temple from a human construction into a celestial abode.

71 TOP - MINIATURE SCALE AND A WEALTH OF DECORATIVE ELEMENTS CHARACTERIZE THE CENTRAL SANCTUARIES OF BANTEAY SREI, WHICH WERE CONSTRUCTED AROUND THE YEAR 967.

71 BOTTOM - THIS SMALL-SCALE REPRODUCTION (H. 37.4 IN.) OF A RELIGIOUS EDIFICE (CA. 967) GIVES US AN IDEA OF THE ELEGANT WORKMANSHIP OF THE STYLE NAMED AFTER THE BANTEAY SREI COMPLEX, WHICH IS QUITE REMOVED FROM THE COSMIC DIMENSIONS OF ANGKOR (NATIONAL MUSEUM, PHNOM PENH).

The sculpture in these monuments has an intrinsic value; it is an art of deep religious meaning, so much so that the statues were brought to life by means of a ceremony called the "opening of the eyes." This is the reason why the sculpture was executed even in places where it could not be seen and satisfied no aesthetic need. The principal statue was the shrine of the spirit of the deceased king that lies on the spot where his ashes were kept. Few statues have remained in their original position, as they were often removed and/or damaged by thieves looking for treasures that may never have existed, and certainly not in the amount expected by the pillagers, since they were represented symbolically. As was in other cultures, in the Khmer civilization the difference in function that lay at the base of the construction of a temple in a religious complex could depend on various needs, three of which were indispensable: devotional, commemorative, and educational.

Just as occurred in India, in Southeast Asia long sequences of bas-relief sculpture on different registers covered the exterior of the temples along the ambulatories customarily used for processions, a common religious practice. Large free-standing sculptures of divinities were probably set inside the places of worship, at the spot where a half-light, carefully gauged in keeping with the diurnal and seasonal cycle, added a note of mystery to the effigies of the gods. The purpose of the smaller statues or representations of everyday objects, as well as the precious objects, that were found in large quantities during archaeological digs, is less clear: probably they were donations to the temple, votive offerings, or personal objects.

While containing a host of evocations and representations, the Hindu temples and Buddhist *stupas* were themselves worshipped as cult objects. Indeed, they can be viewed as microcosms that reproduce the multiplicity of the universe or, as we have seen, the structure of the cosmic mountain of ancient Indian mythology, the abode of the gods as well as the foundation of the world. The life of the community revolved around them, and the very destiny of the entire Khmer nation was based on its principal places of worship. Normally, the facades of the Hindu temples were aligned with the cardinal points, with the towers set in the four directions around a central tower. The layout was square, or sometimes rectangular, the main temple was surrounded by a wall or more than one wall enclosure, and the courtyards connected by roofed corridors that were elaborate accesses: in this way the entire structure resembled a *mandala*, the graphic representation of the multiplicity and circular nature of existence and experience.

72 TOP - THESE HEADS OF *NAGAS* (H. 86 IN., L. 71 IN.) WATCHED OVER THE RUINS OF PREAH KHAN AT ANGKOR (MUSÉE GUIMET, PARIS).

72 BOTTOM - THE AVENUE LEADING TO THE PREAH KHAN, AS IN OTHER COMPLEXES AT ANGKOR, HAD TWO BALUSTRADES IN THE GUISE OF A *NAGA* SUPPORTED BY GIANTS (MUSÉE GUIMET, PARIS).

73 - IN THIS SINGULAR REPRESENTATION (H. 67 IN.) OF A BALUSTRADE, A *NAGA* IS ASSOCIATED WITH THE VULTURE GARUDA (MUSÉE D'INDOCHINE DU TROCADÉRO, PARIS).

74 LEFT - AMONG THE
GUARDIANS OF THE SAFETY
AND PEACE OF THE BANTEAY
SREI TEMPLE THERE WAS THIS
ANTHROPOMORPHIC STATUE
WITH A MONKEY'S HEAD (H.
34.5 IN.; NATIONAL MUSEUM,
PHNOM PENH).

74 RIGHT - ANOTHER
GUARDIAN (H. 35.5 IN.),
WITH THE FEATURES OF A
YAKSA, A GIGANTIC SPIRIT OF
NATURE, WATCHED OVER
THE SITE OF BANTEAY SREI
(NATIONAL MUSEUM, PHNOM
PENH).

This cosmology, for whose construction various building materials were used, depending on the different places and time, can be seen throughout Southeast Asia, without any distinction between the Buddhist complexes (such as the Bayon at Angkor or the Borobudur in Java, or again the Burmese *stupas* at Pagan) and the Hindu ones (such as Angkor Wat). In Khmer Cambodia the cult of the god-king (*devaraja*) was based on the assumption that the sovereign was the mediator and interpreter of divine will and that the images of the god in the temples the king or emperor built symbolized celestial approval of the king's right to rule. While the Hindu rulers chose Shiva or Vishnu as their tutelary gods, thus having themselves represented in the guise of divinities, the Buddhist kings did not refer directly to Buddha (who had renounced all earthly possessions and prestige) but rather to one of the many *bodhisattvas*, who it was believed not only still participated in the life of this world but also possessed extraordinary powers. The third reason for building the temples was to transmit religious teaching, even by means of the appropriate architecture and iconography. In fact, in the interior of an architectural structure that symbolically reproduced the universe, the large narrative reliefs on the walls played an educational role. The Khmer rulers, especially in Cambodia, commissioned very large reliefs on the temple walls that represented historic or hagiographic episodes from the Buddhist tradition together with lively representations of Hindu mythology. In several cases, however, in the typical interaction between the supernatural world and human universe, they also provided a detailed view of the life of the court, the nobles and the commoners, which are precious documents regarding historic events, domestic customs, and productive and artistic activity.

75 - GARUDA IS REPRESENTED IN VARIOUS WAYS. IN THIS STATUE FROM BANTEAY SREI TEMPLE (H. 34 IN., EXECUTED IN THE SECOND HALF OF THE 10TH CENTURY, THE MYTHICAL VULTURE IS ANTHROPOMORPHIC, IN THE GUISE OF A GUARDIAN (NATIONAL MUSEUM, PHNOM PENH).

*3*

# THE APOGEE OF THE KHMER CIVILIZATION

## A NEW CAPITAL

From the outset the Khmer Empire had three essential bases: territorial (centered around the region north of the Tonlé Sap or Great Lake in Cambodia), political (a universal ruler with semi-divine attributes), and religious (Buddhism with marked Hindu characteristics or influences). And all three had their focal point in Angkor, a city that was at once human and divine: the capital of the empire and center of cultural and religious diffusion; the hub of commerce and transportation, as well of cosmic energy and power; the seat of splendid courts, with works that aimed at suggesting the immortality of their builders, immense *memento mori* symbolizing human frailty and mortality. These bases, together with the external contributions made during the historic evolution of this empire, explain its compactness and heterogeneous nature, its strong point and latent fragility. Each of these elements would develop and would eventually create the Khmer civilization, which was dynamic, highly regarded and imitated, but also fraught with conflict and destruction.

Once again, the inscriptions on the steles found in the former imperial territory tell us that the son of Indravarman, Yashovarman I (who ruled from 889 to 900), began his reign with a highly meritorious work that probably earned him the sympathy of the Buddhist world: he built 100 hermitages (*ashra-*

*ma*) for the monks throughout his empire. The only trace we have of these are the dedicatory steles scattered over a territory that ranges from Cambodia to east Thailand and south-central Laos. Like so many other works, the steles provide us with precious information regarding the patrons and the context of their construction, but without mentioning the designers and builders. In a later phase this sovereign concentrated his extraordinary building activity on his small capital, Hariharalaya. Most importantly, he built the ancestral temple of Lolei on the islet in the middle of the Indratataka *baray* his father had built. Lolei consists of four massive brick towers supported by a platform, which is also brick, surrounded by a wall made of blocks of

laterite, a porous and rather friable stone that becomes hard once exposed to the air and sun. According to the texts carved on the sandstone door jambs, the temple was dedicated to Indravarman, who is identified as Shiva. Afterward, having carried out his dynastic duty, as it were, Yashovarman directed his attention to the plain to the west, where he decided to found a new capital on the present-day site of Angkor. This decision was prob-

ably made for various reasons, all of equal importance: strategic, in that it offered greater centrality in an area that was crucial for the empire, more efficacious control of the land and river routes, and the equidistant position between the Great Lake and hills; religious, because the waterways in the region were considered holy; and practical for the abundance of water, the flat land, fertile soil and facility of movement and transportation.

77 - At Angkor Wat, the ideal center of the Khmer world, a female divinity is depicted wearing rich ornaments and jewels.

78 left and 79 top right - The Lolei temple has the best sculpture pieces in the Roluos group, such as these praying

figures in one of the sanctuary towers (left) and the guardian of the gates, the dvarapala, at right.

78-79 and 79 bottom right - Lolei, a temple complex built for Yashovarman I (late 9th century), is known for its combination of bricks and limestone.

The new capital, Yashodharapura ("The City That Bears Glory"), rose up around the temple mountain Phnom Bakheng, on a small oval hill to enhance its symbolic meaning and power. But outside the city Yashovarman had two minor temples built, also in an elevated position: the first, known as Phnom Bok, is situated along a line that connects Phonom Bakheng with Prasat Rong Chen on the Phnom Kulen mountains, the testimony of the foundation of the empire and guarantor of its prosperity; the second, Phnom Krom, lies southward, overlooking the large Tonlé Sap lake.

Phnom Bakheng, probably built in 907, was the largest and most complex temple as yet built by the Khmer. Inside an enclosure wall with embedded shrines, the architects laid out a large pyramid with five terraces that had other small shrines (108 all told, a magic number in Hinduism), with a quincunx of towers on a low platform on the top, four facing the cardinal points and the fifth, tallest one in the middle—a symbolic structure (*mandala*) that refers to the peaks of the mythical Mt. Meru. Inside the main shrine in the middle of the *mandala* was a *linga* dedicated to Shiva as the Yashodhareshvara ("The Lord Who Bears Glory"). Three other elements in the Bakheng state temple became integral parts of Khmer religious architecture.

The first was the access to the complex facing east; the second, the pair of guardian lions placed at the entranceway and, in this case, at the foot of the hill; the third element consists of the two "libraries" (this is the name given to the characteristic low annexes in Khmer architecture with only one chamber that were used by the Buddhists to store the sacred texts and precious objects belonging to the nearby monastic communities, and were probably used for cult purposes by the Hindu priests) that flank the access route to the temple.

Consolidating the tradition by which each king first ordered the building of a grand public work and then, in succession, of his ancestral temple and the state temple, before construction of the Lolei in Indratataka had begun Yashovarman had initiated work on a huge reservoir that was 4.5 miles long and 1 mile wide: the East Baray or Yashodharatataka. Situated to the east of its temple mountain, the East Baray must have been used for both practical and ritual purposes. This was probably the case with all the large *barays*, although the definitive motivation for these works has not yet been clearly identified. For example, there is no trace of these reservoirs in the myriad bas-reliefs that depict in detail so many aspects of life in the Khmer empire.

80 - THE FIRST TEMPLE-MOUNTAIN WITH A QUINCUNX STRUCTURE, PHNOM BAKHENG (H. 220 FT) WAS BUILT BETWEEN THE 9TH AND 10TH CENTURY AT YASHODHARAPURA, IN THE ANGKOR AREA.

81 - A LION GUARDS THE CENTRAL SANCTUARY OF PHNOM BAKHENG. DESPITE THE DAMAGE WROUGHT BY TIME AND NEGLECT, THE COMPLEX HAS RETAINED ITS EPIC AND SYMBOLIC DIMENSION.

82 - INTRICATE DECORATION ADORNS
THE CENTRAL SANCTUARY OF PHNOM
BAKHENG, WHICH WAS DEDICATED TO
THE CULT OF SHIVA.

82-83 - THE CENTRAL SANCTUARY OF
PHNOM BAKHENG IS SURROUNDED BY
FASCIAE THAT MARK OFF THE CORNERS
OF THE BUILDING, DECORATED WITH
FEMALE FIGURES.

After Yashovarman I died around the year 900, he had two direct successors: Harshavarman I (910-923) and Isanavarman II (923-928), brothers who were totally overshadowed by their father's exploits and who left few works, except for the construction on the part of the former of the Baksey Chamkrong, a small brick pyramid temple situated northeast of the Phnom Bakheng, and the Prasat Kravan ("The Cardamom Sanctuary") with its three delicate brick towers, the main one of which houses extraordinary sculptures of Vishnu and his consort Lakshmi.

In 928, Jayavarman IV, a usurper, for reasons unknown to us decided to move the capital to Koh Ker, about 56 miles northeast of Angkor, where he built a splendid complex with hundreds of monuments of varying sizes, many of which are still hidden in the surrounding forest, which is now dangerous because of the many land mines concealed there. He ruled here, in a region rich in mineral resources but relatively arid, for about fifteen years. His reign was recorded in the chronicles of the time and was known to posterity because of the various large stone sculptures of extraordinary workmanship and a fine sense of movement, some of which (including the famous pair of monkey-men engaged in a bitter struggle) are kept in the National Museum of Phnom Penh.

Even after the end of the rather bizarre experience of Jayavarman IV's rule, Angkor must have profited from its highly skilled sculptors, who utilized the sandstone from Koh Ker. The vast royal palace and the reservoir that skirts it to the south, which was hewn out of the rock, are the most important civil works at this site. However, once again it is the state temple, the Prasat Thom, which is so astonishing. Situated west of the royal palace, this monument is an imposing seven-story pyramid topped by a Shivaist shrine that once contained an enormous *linga*.

During the three years of the feckless reign of Harshavarman II after Jayavarman IV died in 941, the empire ran the risk of disintegrating due to the determined attempt of various minor Khmer rulers to break free and become independent.

84 TOP - VISHNU IS DEPICTED IN A PARTICULARLY EXPRESSIVE MANNER ON THE CENTRAL TOWER OF PRASAT KRAVAN.

84 BOTTOM - COLUMNS MADE UP OF OCTAGONAL SECTIONS FRAME THE ENTRANCE TO ONE OF THE PRASAT KRAVAN TOWERS, WHICH DATE FROM THE FIRST HALF OF THE 10TH CENTURY.

84-85 - PRASAT KRAVAN, A MINOR COMPLEX IN ARCHITECTURAL TERMS, WAS MOSTLY REBUILT AND HAD FIVE TOWERS ON A SINGLE PLATFORM.

86 - VERY LITTLE REMAINS
OF THE EDIFICES OF KOH
KER, WHICH ARE
SURROUNDED BY THE
FOREST ABOUT 37 MILES
FROM ANGKOR, AND LITTLE
IS KNOWN ABOUT THE
REASONS WHY IT WAS
CONSTRUCTED.

86-87 - KOH KER, THE CITY
BUILT AT THE BEHEST OF
JAYAVARMAN IV (WHO RULED
FROM 928 TO 944),
REPLACED ANGKOR AS THE
CAPITAL FOR ABOUT TWENTY
YEARS.

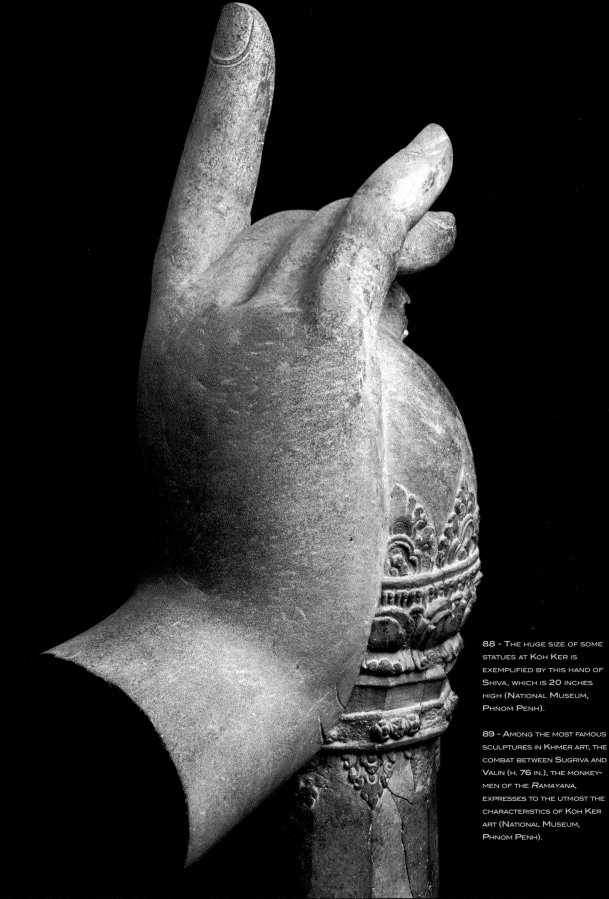

88 - THE HUGE SIZE OF SOME
STATUES AT KOH KER IS
EXEMPLIFIED BY THIS HAND OF
SHIVA, WHICH IS 20 INCHES
HIGH (NATIONAL MUSEUM,
PHNOM PENH).

89 - AMONG THE MOST FAMOUS
SCULPTURES IN KHMER ART, THE
COMBAT BETWEEN SUGRIVA AND
VALIN (H. 76 IN.), THE MONKEY-
MEN OF THE *RAMAYANA*,
EXPRESSES TO THE UTMOST THE
CHARACTERISTICS OF KOH KER
ART (NATIONAL MUSEUM,
PHNOM PENH).

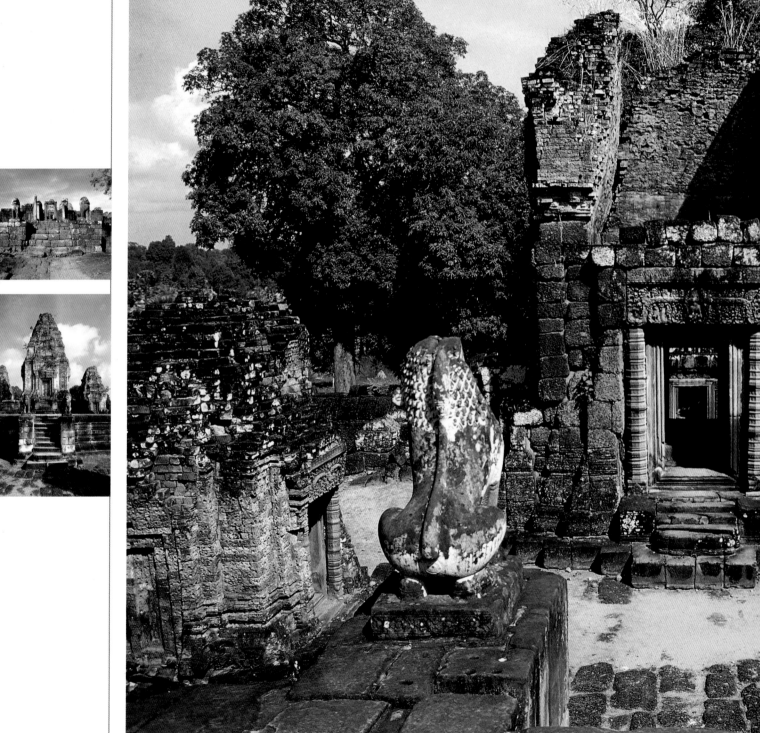

His cousin Rajendravarman II took power and brought the capital back to Yashodharapura in 944 and regained all the territories that had become independent. However, the center of his power was not the area around Phnom Bakheng, but south of the East Baray. Here Rajendravarman II built two major temple mountains. One was the East Mebon, on an island in the middle of the East Baray, and the other Preah Rup, the state temple, which was consecrated in 961 and was also a complex dedicated to Shiva with the typical quincunx layout made of bricks and sandstone. A devout Mahayana Buddhist who nonetheless tolerated the Hindu faith of many of his subjects, Rajendravarman II also built the small Bat Chum temple, dedicated to Buddha.

Only nine years separate the construction of the East Mebon and the Preah Rup, Shivaite temples that have similar layouts, construction and decoration: while the decoration in the former monument is of higher quality, the latter reveals greater balance and lightness from an architectural standpoint. In the Mebon the symbolism of Meru, the mythical mountain that is the abode of the gods and axis of the universe, is underscored by the place-

90 LEFT AND 90-91 - A TEMPLE BUILT BY RAJENDRAVARMAN II (944-968), THE EAST MEBON LIES ON WHAT WAS ONCE AN ISLAND IN THE EAST BARAY AND HIGHLIGHTS THE SYMMETRY AND LIGHTNESS SO CHARACTERISTIC OF THE TEMPLE-MOUNTAINS.

91 - LAKSHMI, THE WIFE OF VISHNU, IS DEPICTED ON THE TOWER (GOPURA) OF THE NORTHEAST ENTRANCE OF THE EAST MEABON WHILE BEING SPLASHED WITH WATER BY ELEPHANTS, ANIMALS THAT ARE A RECURRENT MOTIF IN THIS COMPLEX.

THE FIRST CRISIS AND REBIRTH

HISTORY AND TREASURES OF AN ANCIENT CIVILIZATION

ment of the temple in the middle of the large lake (now a rice paddy) which once contained 1.4 billion cubic feet of water that flowed in from the Siem Reap River. A characteristic feature of the complex is the corner decoration of the first and second levels, with the repeated motif of elephants rendered realistically and with attention to detail. Once again it is the relief sculpture on the towers that renders with marked liveliness and artistic taste the cosmic-mythological vision of the Khmer, which is represented in keeping with the aesthetic canons of a single, unified civilization. Used for funerary purposes and perhaps for this reason given less consideration, the Preah Rup is in a slightly elevated position dominating the East Baray. Of particular interest are the two "libraries" that flank the east entrance to the second lev-

el, which are crowned by tall towers with decorative elements not used elsewhere, such as stone with sculpted representations of the nine planets of Indian astrology and of ascetics. What remains of the stucco decoration on the central towers reveals curious elements: on the southwest tower are an image of Brahmi, the female counterpart of Brahma, and a Vishnu in the unusual reincarnation as a wild boar. Apsaras surround the male images (east towers and central tower) and the female ones (west towers), which were sculpted in the niches.

92-93 - THE PLAN OF THE EAST MEABON IS ONE OF THE MOST COMPLEX OF ALL THE TEMPLE-MOUNTAINS. ITS STRUCTURE IS AN IDEAL REPRODUCTION OF MT. MERU.

93 TOP - THE PREAH RUP HAS THE TYPICAL LAYOUT OF THE KHMER TEMPLE-MOUNTAIN, WHOSE VARIABLE ELEMENTS MAY BE THE SIZE, NUMBER AND FUNCTION OF THE MINOR EDIFICES, ENCLOSURES AND COURTS.

93 BOTTOM - THE FIVE CENTRAL TOWERS OF THE TEMPLE-MOUNTAIN PREAH RUP, NEAR THE EAST BARAY, PRESENT GREAT FORMAL EQUILIBRIUM.

For his ancestral temple he decided to use the ancient Baksei Chamkrong, a modest pyramid temple at the foot of the hill crowned by the majestic Phnom Bakheng; he restored it and placed a gilded statue of Parameshvara (the "Supreme Lord," or Shiva) in the shrine on the top of the pyramid. While the enclosure wall has virtually disappeared except for the remains of a *gopura* with its stairway on the east side, the original features of the pyramid made of laterite and brick (typical 10th-century building materials) have remained practically intact, beginning with the size: the structure measures 88 ft per side at the base and 49 ft on the top, and is 43 ft high, divided into four stories with four narrow stairways at the cardinal points that ascend from the base to the apex. The shrine on the top is more impressive than the rest of the monument; it is 26 ft per side, and the only true entrance lies on the east side. The blind doors at the other cardinal points, with the decorative lintels and thin columns, are the only elements made of sandstone and are filled with decorative carvings and inscriptions that trace the genealogy of the king back to the mythical ascetic Kambu, to whom Shiva gave a celestial nymph, or *apsara*, as his bride. Their progeny (*Kambu-ja*) would be the Khmer and, by extension, the present-day Cambodians.

Rajendravarman II's victorious struggle against the Cham has epic overtones, and by 968, the year of his death, his military campaigns had guaranteed a certain degree of security at the borders of his empire. This allowed his adolescent son, Jayavarman V, to succeed him and inaugurate a long reign (968-1001) marked by important architectural works. Particularly remarkable among these are the Shivaist complex of Banteay Srei ("Citadel of the Women"), which was begun by his father but officially dedicated to Shiva at the beginning of his reign by his

counselor, the Brahmin Yajñavaraha, and the impressive temple mountain of Takeo. Banteay Srei, located 14 miles from the middle of Angkor, is a true jewel of Khmer architecture both for its reduced, almost miniaturized size (the entrances to the edifices are no more than 4 ft high) and for the marvelous decoration and sculpture that adorn it and that remind one more of wooden structures than stone ones. These are expressions of a fully mature art that here more than anywhere else drew inspiration from the Indian models but by no means imitated them. Restored by the French missions, which adopted the anastylosis technique for the first time at Angkor, the site was favored from the outset by the red sandstone quarries at nearby Phnom Kulen and the deposits of laterite in the vicinity that, curiously enough, did not induce the builders to create a large work. Since Banteay Srei was dedicated to the cult of Shiva, its main entrance faces east. Access to the *sancta sanctorum* is had by going through a straight ceremonial causeway flanked by pavilions that leads to a *gopura* set into the first enclosure wall and which in turn leads to the median part of the complex; a second roofless passageway and portal-pavilion in the second wall afford access to the central part of the complex. This latter includes three large shrines—the main, central one which once housed a large *linga*—as well as two "libraries" and some minor edifices. While the architectural structures are remarkable, the fame of this complex is due mostly to its sculpture: the almost free-standing guardians (*dvarapala*) and goddesses (*devata*) that flank the doors and were also carved on the outer walls, as well as the episodes from the *Purana* and from the epic poems that decorate the tympana in complex sequences and that seem to have difficulty imposing themselves among the plant motif decoration that covers every inch of the entire central part of the complex.

96 - OF REDUCED SIZE BUT WITH PERFECT PROPORTIONS AND DETAILS, THE HUMAN FIGURES (SUCH AS THIS WOMAN ON THE MAIN SHRINE) IN THE BANTEAY SREI ARE AMONG THE BEST IN KHMER ART.

97 TOP - THE BAS-RELIEFS AND OTHER SCULPTURE WORK AT BANTEAY SREI ARE IN KEEPING WITH THE CONSOLIDATED TECHNIQUES AND INSPIRATION OF THE KHMER REPERTOIRE, BUT ALSO REVEAL A TASTE FOR DETAIL AND TECHNICAL MASTERY.

97 BOTTOM - SYMBOLIC AND MYTHOLOGICAL NARRATION COVERS MOST OF THE BUILDINGS, TOGETHER WITH STYLIZED PLANT MOTIFS, ESPECIALLY IN THE CENTRAL SECTION.

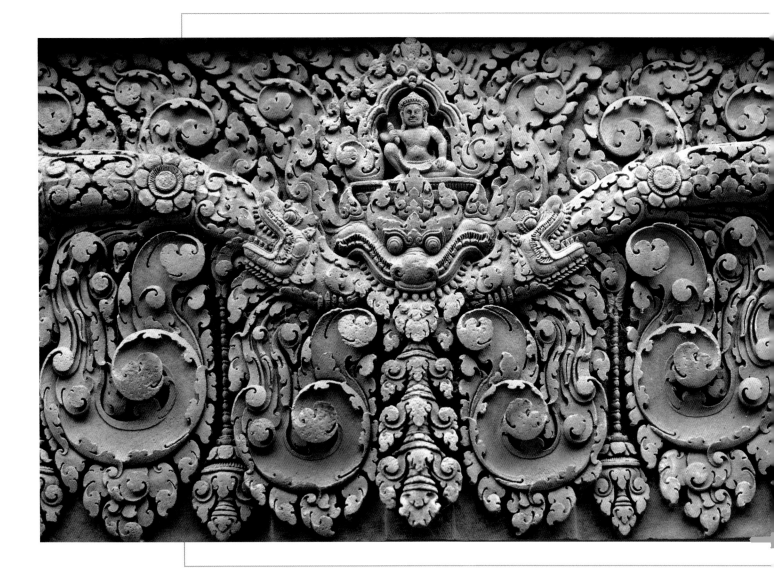

98 - Kala, defeated by Shiva who here towers over him, is an all-devouring demon who is used to guard holy places, decorates an entrance of Banteay Srei.

99 - Kala holding two nagas in his jaws is a common motif in Khmer art, and was executed at Banteay Srei with a wealth of details.

While Banteay Srei is the monument to the fervid faith and profound knowledge of the multiform Hindu universe of Yajñavaraha, it is also a tribute to the king's religious tolerance. Just like his father, who was a Buddhist, he most willingly flanked his devotion to the already rich Mahayana pantheon with elements from the cult of Shiva and Vishnu. The Takeo, his state temple, was erected on the west bank of the East Baray. Unlike Banteay Srei, which is all measure and equilibrium in an "anthology" of architectural and decorative elements, the 72 ft high Takeo is a monument with the characteristic quincunx form made entirely of sandstone, one of the most impressive works of Khmer architecture. But its distinguishing feature is that it is unfinished, or at least, this is the impression one has of the totality of this work, which is so simple and almost lacking in decoration. According to the legend carved in an inscription, the monument was struck by lightning while it was being built, and this event, considered ominous, led the builders to stop construction.

The death of Jayavarman V in the year 1000 closed a fecund chapter in the history of Angkor and also ended the direct royal lineage that had begun with Rajendravarman. After

the brief interregnum of Udayadityavarman, the Khmer world fell into a state of anarchy and violence. The bloody, nine-year dispute between two rival princes, one based at Angkor and the other in eastern Cambodia, for the right to ascend the throne of Angkor and to claim the supreme title of *chakravartin* ("Lord of the Wheel", or "Universal Ruler") ended with the victory of the latter, who assumed the throne name of Suryavarman I (1002-1050). This great but obscure personage asserted he came from a royal family of Nakhon Si Thammarat (now southern Thailand, at the time an area that was probably under Javanese dominion), but historical sources are contradictory and the king's affirmation was probably aimed at justifying his expansionist policy and his claims over territories far from the original Khmer lands. What is certain is that Suryavarman I reorganized and strengthened the empire administration, created a system of domestic security, and acquired further prestige by extending his borders northward on to part of southern Laos, and southward in the peninsular region of Thailand, giving the Khmer control of the Gulf of Thailand and the sea routes of Indochina. In order to achieve this objective, several times he led his armies against the Mon kingdom, which controlled central and southern Thailand, eventually annexing it around the year 1025. The conquest and the elevation to the rank of

provincial capital of Lavo (present-day Lop Buri), a major Mon city, meant that Suryavarman I could now control the lower course of the Chao Phraya River and consolidate Khmer economic dominance over most of Southeast Asia. Indeed, under this king Khmer power attained its maximum territorial expansion.

However, memory of this sovereign is also due to his achievements as a great builder and reformer. His royal palace, a rectangle 1,970 ft long and 820 ft wide surrounded by thick walls 20 ft high, was for centuries the king's residence and as well as the fulcrum of the imperial administrative system.

100 LEFT - UNFINISHED FOR REASONS UNKNOWN TO US, TAKEO GIVES THE IMPRESSION OF MAJESTY, WHICH IS ACCENTUATED BY ITS VERTICAL THRUST AND THE SCARCITY OF ACCOMPANYING ARCHITECTURAL ELEMENTS.

100-101 - A RECTANGULAR, AND NOT SQUARE, PLAN, WITH THE TOWERS IN A QUINCUNX LAYOUT ON THREE TIERS: ONCE AGAIN, MYTHICAL MT. MERU WAS THE MODEL FOR THE ARCHITECTS.

101 BOTTOM - SIMPLICITY AND STATELINESS ARE THE MAIN FEATURES OF TAKEO, A TEMPLE-MOUNTAIN BUILT IN THE 10TH-11TH CENTURY.

Determined to be the absolute center of the life of the empire, Suryavarman I chose a central area near his apartment inside the palace enclosure as the site for his ancestral temple, Phimeanakas. This unusual choice was justified, according to tradition, by the nocturnal visits the king made to the gilded tower that presumably once stood on the top of the sacred structure. Here, by lying with a divinity that was part woman and part reptile with nine heads, Suryavarman supposedly revived the primordial alliance between the Khmer and the spirits of the earth. Land and water once again formed an indivisible combination, a pair of natural elements whose control justified the king's power and enhanced his possessions. Only one more work was lacking to ensure the immortality of the figure of Suryavarman I. The magnificence of the West Baray was intended to remain unsurpassed; five miles long and with a maximum width of one mile and a capacity of around 13 billion gallons of water, this reservoir was of a truly superhuman, almost cosmic size. This grandiose work alone, which was probably completed by Suryavarman I's successor, Udayadityavarman II, would by itself have been enough to immortalize this emperor. But it was Preah Vihear, an architectural achievement that was spectacular for its position and structure, a complex of

great artistic importance, that ensured lasting fame for Suryavarman I, who completed the construction that had probably begun in 893 and was continued by several kings.

This Shivaite complex stands on a rocky cliff of the Dangrek range, which separates the Cambodian plain from the Khorat plateau that now marks the border between Cambodia and Thailand. This temple extends for 2600 ft over a single North-South course that winds its way among several courtyards by means of a series of five elaborate entrance pavilions (gopura) with access stairways up to the end shrine, which dominates the plain from an escarpment over 1,650 ft high.

The most ancient surviving parts date from the time when the capital of the Khmer empire was Koh Ker, while the more recent ones date to the 12th century. The fifth gopura (really the first if one enters from the opposite side, following the correct chronological order, up to the first gopura, which is really the last one) still bears traces of the original painting. The fourth and next pavilion has a minor masterpiece on the south side of its base: a bas-relief sculpture depicting the Churning of the Ocean of Milk. The third and largest gopura is flanked by two edifices (which may have once been used as hostels for pilgrims) and probably afforded access to the area the king normally used as his residence when on visit here.

It is by no means easy to render the attraction and fascination of this site or recover its symbolic meaning. What we can say with certainty is that, with its symmetry, beauty, placement in the natural setting and state of preservation, Preah Vihear is an exceptional monument to the grandeur of an empire and to the foresight of the kings who had it built. After his death in 1049, Suryavarman I, who for his entire reign had manifested his preference for Shivaite Hinduism, received the posthumous title of Nirvanapada ("He Who Has Attained Enlightenment"). This was only natural in a period in which the king was still considered the defender of Buddhist law, and Mahayana Buddhism was so strong that it could afford to assimilate many elements of Hinduism without losing its identity, and actually was enriched by the addition of new iconographic influences and ceremonial modes.

102-103 - THE THIRD ENTRANCE PAVILION, OR GOPURA, STANDS ALONG THE AVENUE LEADING TO THE CENTRAL SHRINE OF PREAH VIHEAR.

103 RIGHT - AMONG THE VARIOUS ARCHITECTURAL ELEMENTS AT PREAH VIHEAR, WHICH WAS A PILGRIMAGE SITE, THERE IS A POOL USED FOR ABLUTIONS.

After a period marked by the reign of several minor kings, it was Suryavarman II who resumed contact with the glorious Khmer tradition. However, mention should be made of one sovereign who preceded him, Udayadityavarman II, whose greatest achievement was the construction, around the year 1060, of the Baphuon, the immense temple mountain that was his state temple. This was the largest religious edifice of the time, surpassed about one century later only by the magnificence of Angkor Wat, and it is also one of the most significant achievements of Khmer architecture. This temple was built in the heart of the ancient capital, standing against the south wall of the royal palace. It is distinguished by the great number of bas-relief panels that for the most part drew inspiration from the epic poems *Ramayana* and *Mahabharata*. In their eagerness to construct a colossal work, the builders ended up creating one of the most fragile monuments at Angkor. In fact, the temple was built around three huge superposed stone galleries filled with sand, a building technique that was devised at Angkor and also utilized in preceding periods. However, the sheer size of the Baphuon, which is 425 × 340 ft at the base and almost 130 ft high, was the fundamental cause of the problems that arose. The weight of the sand proved to be too much for the thin retaining walls that formed the three levels. Furthermore, the water that infiltrated the stones added to the weight, causing entire sections of the walls to collapse, especially during the devastating monsoons of 1943.

French archaeologists and engineers endeavored to restore the monument in the 1960s, and their work continued amid tremendous difficulties later. However, in recent years the gradual reconstruction led to partial reopening of the complex in 2006 (985 ft of the east façade, as well as a causeway that allows visitors to see the huge reclining 230 ft Buddha sculpted on the lowest terrace of Baphoun from the 15th century, when the original structure underwent drastic changes in order to convert it into a Theravada Buddhist sanctuary). Reconstruction of the central part of the complex should be finished by 2008, which would restore to the world one of the key monuments in Angkor. Indeed, the work being done on the Baphuon is the largest and most enterprising restoration ever undertaken on Khmer monuments, an achievement that is even more significant if we take into account the fact that it was based almost totally on the great number of photographs taken of the site in the early 20th century. By using these photos and the few sections of the outer enclosure walls still standing, the archaeologists succeeded in determining the original position of all the stones scattered around the site (about 300,000 all told), beginning with the series of decorative friezes. Indeed, rather than restoration, this is an actual reconstruction, which has obliged the technicians of the École Française d'Extrême-Orient (EFEO) to overcome many engineering problems.

The other great project that is traditionally ascribed to Udayadityavarman was the construction of the dikes to regulate the flow of the water in the West Baray, and the artificial island with its temple in the middle of the West Mebon—the only well-preserved parts of which are the towers on the east side—which was also famous in ancient times for having housed a colossal bronze statue of Shiva lying on his side during the creation of the universe. The only remaining part of this work, which is rightly considered one of the largest bronze sculptures in all Southeast Asia, is a section of the torso with the head and two arms (4 ft high and 7 ft wide) now kept in the National Museum in Phnom Penh.

104 TOP - THE BAPHUON TEMPLE CONTAINS EXTRAORDINARY BAS-RELIEF SCULPTURE, MOST OF WHICH WAS APPLIED ONTO THE MONUMENT, A TECHNIQUE THAT WAS LATER ABANDONED BY THE KHMER ARTISTS AND ARCHITECTS.

104 BOTTOM - BAPHUON, ONE OF THE LEADING DYNASTIC TEMPLES, IS STILL UNDERGOING RADICAL RESTORATION WORK. HERE WE SEE THE *GOPURA* THAT AFFORDS ACCESS TO THE CENTRAL SANCTUARY.

105 - THE CENTRAL SANCTUARY OF BAPHUON, WITH ITS WEALTH OF ARCHITECTURAL AND SCULPTED ELEMENTS, IS ONE OF THE MOST ENDANGERED PARTS OF THE COMPLEX BECAUSE OF ITS INSTABILITY.

Udayadityavarman was succeeded first by his brother Harshavarman III, whose fourteen-year reign was marked by domestic difficulties and the first defeat suffered at the hands of the Cham, and then by Jayavarman VI. This latter king, who was probably a noble vassal who hailed from the region of Khorat, in northeast Thailand, took power by defeating his predecessor in battle. He did very little to augment the glory of Angkor, but in his native land he built one of the largest archaeological complexes in Southeast Asia, Vimayapura (present-day Phimai), on the upper course of the Mun River. Situated in a region inhabited since the Bronze Age, under

Jayavarman VI Phimai became a minor Angkor, the flourishing provincial capital of the powerful Khmer empire, carefully laid out with a gridiron plan. Its importance is revealed by the major road, 185 miles long, that linked it with Angkor, the principal and best maintained of the communication routes that radiated from the capital. Phimai was in such a safe position that it had no need of walls until a much later period, during the reign of Jayavarman VII. The principal religious complex there, Prasat Hin Phimai, has an unusual alignment, on the North-South axis of the city instead of the East-West one, and faces south (or better, southeast, the direction of Angkor, which may have been a prudent tribute to the proud capital of the empire) instead of east. As was the case with Suryavarman I, Jayavarman VI did not allow his Buddhist beliefs to obstruct the flourishing of Hindu iconography, which is to be found together with Mahayana motifs in the decoration of the temple complex, as well as in the many skillfully wrought statues and everyday objects found in digs and now mostly kept in the large and well organized national museum in the city.

Unlike Angkor, where the relative state of abandon has preserved the ancient urban structures, at Phimai these can only be seen in aerial photographs. Thanks to this technique, archaeologists were able to reconstruct the original layout of the

residential area and also discovered that to the south of the city there was a rather large reservoir in the middle of which was an island temple. The pride and joy of present-day Phimai, and most probably of ancient Vimayapura as well, is certainly the Prasat Hin, a double concentric temple complex, each part of which has its own elaborate cruciform entrance pavilion (*gopura*) with images from Vishnuite or Shivaite mythology and episodes from the life of Buddha carved on the lintels. The one facing south is preceded by a gallery guarded by sculpted *nagas* and lions. A characteristic feature of the central sanctuary (*prang*) is the light-colored sandstone tower with an innovative shape that reminds one of a pineapple, a motif that was later used at Angkor and, after further development, in the Thai tem-

ples. In the interior, barely visible in the half-light, is a statue of Buddha meditating while being protected by a *naga*. The Phimai complex was innovative because of its special entrance pavilion as well as for other elements. In the first place, the edifice outside the south entrance (Phlab Phla Pleuang Khreung) is rectangular and has an East-West alignment. This is commonly thought to have been used by the king and his court officials to prepare themselves before entering the sacred area. In the second place, the characteristic quincunx structure is lacking. In fact, around the main tower there are only three other tower structures, each one with a different shape: Prang Brahmadat, Prang Hin Daeng, and Klang Ngoen. Other edifices are the "library" (*panalai*), the sermon hall, and the Brahman's pavilion.

106 TOP - PHIMAI MAY HAVE BEEN THE FIRST ARCHITECTURAL COMPLEX TO USE THE "PINEAPPLE"-LIKE ROOF OF THE MAIN SANCTUARY, WHICH WAS LATER ADOPTED AT ANGKOR.

106 CENTER - THE TEMPLE OF PRASAT HIN LIES IN THE MIDDLE OF THE PHIMAI COMPLEX, IN THAILAND, THE LARGEST ONE OUTSIDE CAMBODIA.

106 BOTTOM - THE NAGAS, MANY-HEADED SERPENTS IN

HINDU MYTHOLOGY THAT BECAME GUARDIANS IN BUDDHIST ICONOGRAPHY, ARE A COMMON MOTIF IN KHMER ART.

106-107 - STONE LIONS GUARD THE AVENUE LEADING TO THE PRASAT HIN. DESPITE SOME HINDU ELEMENTS, PHIMAI WAS BUDDHIST FROM THE OUTSET.

108-109 - AN ALMOST CARICATURAL KALA ON A FRAGMENT OF A LINTEL KEPT IN THE PHIMAI MUSEUM.

## THE COMMUNICATION ROUTES

There is an aspect of Khmer civilization that is little known and has hardly been studied, partly because of the difficulty involved in gaining a clear overall view of a civilization that is made up of humans and not just of stones. This is the remarkable Khmer road network, which must have been of crucial importance for such a large and populous empire that lay in the middle of a region that was privileged from very ancient times by having land and sea connections between West and South Asia on the one hand and East Asia on the other.

There are at least six large arteries that have been somewhat preserved and are still used to some extent. Two of these ran southward: the first from Angkor to Kompong Thom, for about 90 miles, skirting the Tonlé Sap lake to the east; the second headed east to Preah Khan via Beng Mealea (60 miles). From there a spur led to Wat Phu, in Laos, passing through Koh Ker (130 miles); another to the south went toward the Great Lake for 25 miles; northward, a road whose final stretch can hardly be seen now went to Banteay Chhmar (37 miles), while the largest road built by the Khmer crossed the Dangrek mountain range before descending onto the Khorat plateau and reaching Phimai after a 130 mile run.

Besides the width, which ranged from 33 to 82 ft, one feature of these Khmer "highways" was that they were partly elevated, sometimes as much as 20 ft, in order to counter the period flooding caused by monsoons. These stretches of elevated road were part of the vast system adopted to control the flow of water, acting as barriers during the periods of heavy rainfall and, by means of wells and small catchments placed in the structure, preserving this precious liquid in the dry season. Bridges and stop-off areas were an integral and qualifying part of these major roads, which in turn were the hub of a network of minor communication routes. About fifty bridges still survive, some of which are still used by pedestrians and traffic today, including motor vehicles. These are massive structures made of laterite blocks that must have flanked fixed wooden bridges or floating ones. At regular intervals along the roads there were way stations for travelers that probably included the so-called Houses of Fire, 121 structures built at the behest of Jayavarman VII whose actual purpose is still uncertain. They may have been rest houses or sorts of chapels for the celebration of rituals. The kind of traffic that used these roads is shown in the Angkor relief carvings: pedestrians and animals, as well as two-wheel chariots and elephants, retinues of slaves carrying goods, religious processions and military parades, and magnificent parades of royal chariots that looked like mythical palaces. These were major communication routes, multifunctional structures used both for civil and military purposes, as well as to control the water and act as a sort of social service.

110 - THE SCULPTURAL DECORATION OF THE BAYON INCLUDES A WAR CHARIOT ACCOMPANYING THE MARCHING KHMER ARMY.

111 - THIS PANEL WITH A MYTHOLOGICAL THEME IS PART OF THE BAS-RELIEFS OF BAPHUON, OFTEN ASSOCIATED WITH SCENES OF EVERYDAY LIFE.

# UNDER THE SHADOW OF ANGKOR

Suryavarman II ascended the throne in 1113, wresting power from his old great-uncle Dharanindravarman I, the elder brother of Jayavarman VI. His long reign, which lasted until 1150, was distinguished by its military power, political stability and artistic splendor. The establishment of diplomatic relations with Sung Dynasty China in 1116 (which at the same time acknowledged formal Khmer vassalage to the Chinese emperors) was accompanied by military expeditions against the Dai Viet of North Vietnam (ten years of uninterrupted land and sea campaigns that were in vain) and against their neighbors to the south, the Cham, over whom Suryavarman imposed a fragile supremacy in the final years of his reign. In 1145, Khmer troops sacked the Cham capital, Vijaya, as is attested in two relief sculptures at Angkor Wat: one shows the king leading his troops while on an elephant's back and surrounded by his officers, while in the other he is seated on an elaborate throne. The Cham soon got their revenge, but for the moment the Khmer ruler could dedicate the last years of his reign to the construction of stupendous religious edifices. A devotee of Vishnu, Suryavarman II dedicated the new temple of Banteay Samré to this divinity, on the southeast corner of the West Baray, and again at Angkor began construction of one of the architectural wonders of the world, Angkor Wat; he died before he could see the completed work and could participate in the religious dedication ceremony.

Before devoting his fame and most of the empire's resources to such a challenging and demanding work, the construction of which lasted about thirty years, Suryavarman II had two other monumental works built in localities quite a distance from the capital. The first of these was the vast complex of Beng Mealea (whose bastions are 150 ft wide and have an overall length of 2.5 miles) at the base of the Phnom Kulen mountain. The architectural features of this monument made it a probable model, together with Prasat Hin Phimai, for Angkor Wat, which is quite similar in its plan, harmonious composition, and the accentuated monumentality of the vast surfaces with their austere decoration. The second work is Phnom Rung, a Shivaite complex built on the top of a small extinct volcano in present-day Thailand, on the royal road that connected Angkor and Phimai. It was built by a local ruler, probably a relative of Suryavarman II, Narendraditya. The position of this monument makes it one of the few "high places" of Khmer civilization, the legacy of a local tradition of considering the mountains a point where energy was concentrated and where one could be closer to holiness. Because of its structure, this complex–which does not appear to have been part of an urban area or expressly used for cult worship,

while it may have had a dynastic function–seems to have been a pilgrimage site, although it may have been part of a residential area that has left few traces of its existence. A particularly important aspect of this site is the irrigation system, in the center of which are three large *barays*, a sign that the locality could have supported a large population.

Because of its features, Phnom Rung can be placed in an intermediate position between Phimai and Angkor Wat, and in fact is similar in some respects to these two sites: the causeway of the *nagas*, for example, or the *prang* (temple tower)–which is similar to those at Phimai but has interesting differences, including the triangular shape of the tower and the vestibule between the pavilion connecting the external part of the complex and the actual sanctuary. While the entrance to the main tower faces East, as was customary, the entire complex seems to have been planned not so much as a representation of the stereotyped and ascetic cosmogony, but rather as a structure intended as a pleasant abode for the god of the destruction and rebirth of the uni-

verse. The central shrine can be reached by means of a long 525 ft gallery flanked by pillars in the shape of lotus buds. The final part of the passage enters a *gopura* built in the Phimai style. The decoration, which is to be found in various areas of the complex, includes very lively representations that are interesting for the overall unity among some of the elements.

For example, there is the episode from the *Ramayana* sculpted above the west lintel of the main sanctuary, which represents a temple that is nothing more or less than Phnom Rung itself depicted in the shape of a chariot that soars in the air, surrounded by an army of monkeys led by Hanuman and other beings during the battle. What remains of the trident at the top of the sanctuary can barely be made out, since it has deteriorated with time. The tympanum on the east *gopura* shows a bearded Shiva with the so-called inverted trident headdress, wearing an as-

cetic's garb and seated in a yoga position. This might really be a portrait of Narendraditya himself, the builder of the temple. In any case, the image confirms this ruler's Shivaite faith, which is amply demonstrated in other sculpted images of Shiva in the complex, together with rare images of Vishnu. This image of Shi-va-Narendraditya is particularly efficacious and lively, despite the fact that the widespread damage caused by time and pillagers has almost totally erased the images of celestial beings and nymphs that once surrounded it. At the base of the tympanum, a singular male figure is framed by numerous female figures, probably noble women or perhaps even queens. In another area, a pediment has what seems to be a rite of passage into adult-hood rendered in typical 13th-century context and style: a young woman standing, an official seated and flanked by an as-sistant, and a figure that might be one of the woman's relatives.

112 - ON THE SUMMIT OF A SMALL VOLCANIC CONE, PRASAT PHNOM RUNG, NOW IN THAILAND, WAS AN IMPORTANT CITY ON THE ROAD BETWEEN ANGKOR AND PHIMAI. HERE WE SEE A *PRANG* (TOWER) IN THE CENTRAL SANCTUARY.

113 TOP - ALMOST TOTALLY RECONSTRUCTED, BANTEAY SAMRÉ (MID-12TH CENTURY) LIES, STYLISTICALLY SPEAKING, SOMEWHERE BETWEEN THE ANGKOR WAT AND BAYON MODES.

113 BOTTOM - BANTEAY SAMRÉ, A VISHNUITE COMPLEX DATING FROM THE FIRST HALF OF THE 12TH CENTURY, IS ONE OF THE TEMPLES IN THE ANGKOR AREA THAT HAS BEEN RESTORED.

Despite its name (*wat* is a Thai word for a Buddhist temple) Angkor Wat (the City-Temple) was also laid out as an expression of the king's devotion to the Hindu divinity Vishnu, and only in a much later period, when the grandeur of Angkor was coming to an end, did it become a Buddhist temple. Situated in the southeastern part of the city built by Yashovarman I, Angkor Wat is surrounded by a moat that is 5,600 ft long from East to West, 4,900 ft long from North to South, and 650 ft wide. On a sort of island connected to the "terra firma" by a stone causeway guarded by *nagas*, the area inside the laterite enclosure wall around the shrine measures about 52 acres. The complex consists of a series of concentric rectangular courtyards covered with galleries or terraces with open spaces between them that are in turn connected by cruciform galleries. The main entrance lies to the West, and access is gained by way of a broad causeway over the moat made of massive blocks of sandstone. By crossing through a cruciform terrace and going up a stairway, one enters the outermost of the three concentric galleries, known as the Third Gallery, which is famous for its many bas-reliefs. Going past the two following galleries by way of roofed corridors, one arrives at the temple proper, with its tall towers in a quincunx layout, the terrestrial reproduction of the five peaks of Mt. Meru. The huge central tower, which can be ascended to the top, once had a statue of Vishnu, which later disappeared. Or it may have been stolen, as is the case, unfortunately, with most of the monuments in the city, which have lost the small precious objects and gold leaf usually hidden in an excavated area under the statue of the god to whom the Khmer temples were dedicated. The purpose of these objects was to produce energy rather than demonstrate the munificence of the king or represent a precious homage to the god. In the case of Angkor Wat, in 1934 French archaeologists discovered two fragments of crystal and two pieces of gold leaf buried deep inside the laterite foundations.

114 TOP - AT THE FOOT OF THE WEST FAÇADE OF ANGKOR WAT, THE AVENUE IS GUARDED BY A STONE LION.

114 BOTTOM - A LARGE AND ELABORATE *GOPURA* STANDS AT THE END OF THE AVENUE LEADING TO THE COMPLEX, FLANKED BY A BALUSTRADE.

114-115 - THIS AERIAL VIEW OF ANGKOR WAT SHOWS THE CAUSEWAY OVER THE MOAT; THE *GOPURA*; THE ACCESS TO THE CENTRAL AREA FLANKED BY TWO "LIBRARIES"; THREE CONCENTRIC TIERS, THE FIRST TWO OF WHICH HAVE GALLERIES WITH BAS-RELIEF SCULPTURE; AND FIVE TOWERS IN A QUINCUNX PATTERN ON THE TOP PLATFORM.

116-117 - A GROUP OF CELESTIAL NYMPHS (*APSARAS*) WELCOMES VISITORS AT THE ENTRANCE TO THE FIRST BAS-RELIEF GALLERY.

117 TOP AND CENTER - ROOFED GALLERIES CONNECT THE THREE PLATFORMS OF ANGKOR WAT. WITH THE EXCEPTION OF A FEW VIEWPOINTS, IT IS VERY DIFFICULT TO HAVE AN OVERALL VIEW OF THIS COMPLEX AND ITS FIVE CENTRAL TOWERS.

117 BOTTOM - THE WINDOWS, WITH THEIR DELICATE SLENDER STONE COLUMNS, ARE A COMMON FEATURE OF KHMER ARCHITECTURE AND ARE AN IMPORTANT ELEMENT HERE AS WELL.

118-119 - *APSARAS* WITH ELABORATE HAIRDOS REFLECT THE FEATURES AND ATTIRE OF THE DANCERS OR LADIES-IN-WAITING IN THE KHMER COURT.

120-121 AND 120 BOTTOM - THE CHURNING OF THE OCEAN OF MILK, ONE OF THE BASIC MYTHS OF HINDUISM, IS PART OF THE GALLERY OF BAS-RELIEFS ON THE FIRST LEVEL OF ANGKOR WAT. THE FOCAL POINT OF THIS AWESOME CREATIVE WORK IS MT. MANDARA RESTING ON THE TURTLE, BEING SPUN BY THE SERPENT VASUKI UNDER THE SUPERVISION OF VISHNU AND PULLED BY GODS AND DEMONS (BOTTOM LEFT). AT ONE END OF THE SCENE, THE DEMON RAVANA IS SUPPORTING THE HEAD OF THE SERPENT VASUKI (TOP), WHILE BEHIND HIM IS THE ARMY OF DEMONS WITH HORSES AND ELEPHANTS (BOTTOM LEFT).

121 - THE THIRD GALLERY OF ANGKOR WAT BOASTS SPLENDID RELIEF SCULPTURE.

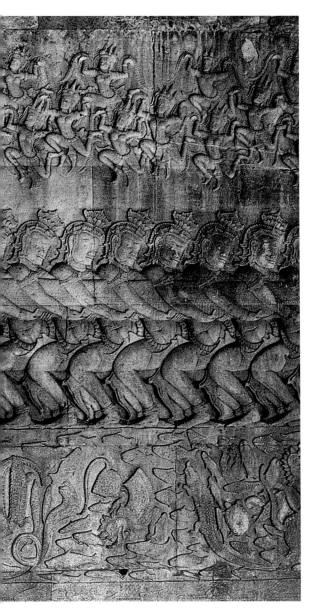

were added in the 16th century. Without taking into account these latter ones, the bas-relief panels extend for 2,300 ft and are 6.5 ft high, which makes them the longest sequence of stone sculpture in the world. Almost without interruption, thousands of figures relate Hindu epics, episodes from the *Purana*, and the tranquil court life as well as the bloody military campaigns of Suryavarman II's reign.

The following is the sequence of the bas-relief sculpture cycles, starting from the south side (thus to the right) of the west gallery, where the main entrance lies:

– the Battle of Kurukshetra, the climax of the entire Hindu epic *Mahabharata*, with the struggle between the rival clans of the Pandava and Kaurava;

– the historic procession presided by Suryavarman II, who is indicated here by the posthumous name of Paramavishnuloka ("He who has attained the reign of the Supreme Vishnu"). The vivacious sequence includes Brahmins, court ladies, a parade of horsemen and infantrymen of the army, with their commanders (including the king) riding elephants, and Thai mercenaries;

– Heavens and Hells, including the punishment meted out to the damned in the kingdom of Yama, the god of death;

– the Churning of the Ocean of Milk, the fundamental event in the story of creation as elaborated by Hindu mythology. The bas-reliefs offer an outstanding and spectacular description (and in fact this cycle is considered one of the absolute masterpieces of Khmer art) of the churning of the primordial cosmic water, which is effected by placing Mt. Mandara on the back of an enormous tortoise and wrapping the giant *naga* Vasuki around the mountain like a rope; then gods and demons pull at either end, thus causing the mountain to rotate and churn the waters, which produces the elixir of immortality as well as most of the living and mythological creatures;

– Vishnu's victory over the demons (*asura*), one the most recent reliefs, together with the following one, which relates Khrishna's victory over the demon Bana;

– the battle between gods and demons, in which the 21 leading gods of the Hindu pantheon participate, each one riding on his typical mount;

– the Battle of Lanka, in which Rama and his allies, the army of monkeys, defeat the demon Ravana and rescue Rama's consort Sita, who has been kidnapped by Ravana. This episode from the *Ramayana* is also sculpted on the corner pavilions.

The grandiosity associated with the equilibrium of the architectural elements and its highly fascinating setting, which is at once artificial and natural, have earned lasting fame for Angkor Wat, while the stupendous sequence of bas-reliefs in the main (or third) gallery is an inestimable testimony of artistic capability and cultural synthesis. It also provides a precise representation of many aspects of Khmer civilization that would otherwise have been unknown to us.

Most of the bas-reliefs are quite beautiful and lively. Exceptions are the ones in the northeastern corner, which

122 LEFT - COMMON PEOPLE PAY
TRIBUTE TO A HIGH-RANKING PERSON IN
THIS SCENE FROM THE JUDGMENT OF
THE DEAD RELIEF IN THE THIRD
GALLERY OF ANGKOR WAT.

122 RIGHT - A PRINCESS ON A
PALANQUIN PARTICIPATES IN THE
JUDGMENT OF THE DEAD AND FOLLOWS
THE PROCESSION THAT WILL TAKE HER TO
PARADISE.

122-123 - SURYAVARMAN II, SEATED ON
HIS THRONE AND FLANKED BY FAN-
BEARERS, PRESIDES OVER THE HISTORIC
PROCESSION IN THE MAIN GALLERY AT
ANGKOR WAT.

124-125 - IN THE JUDGMENT
OF YAMA, THE ASCENT TO
HEAVEN OF THE RIGHTEOUS IS
CORRESPONDED BY THE
DESCENT TO HELL OF THE
WRONGDOERS, SYMBOLIZING
RESPECTIVELY ACCESS TO A
SUPERIOR COSMIC ORDER AND
THE RETURN TO THE
PRIMORDIAL CHAOS.

126-127 - THE KHMER ARMY
MARCHING IN A DETAIL FROM
THE BAS-RELIEF SCULPTURE
THAT DECORATES THE SOUTH
GALLERY OF ANGKOR WAT.

128-129 - THE ARMY,
CONSISTING OF INFANTRYMEN
AND LIGHT CAVALRY, MARCHES
TO THE FINAL BATTLE ON THE
FIELD OF KURUKSHETRA.
DESPITE THE SEEMINGLY
STATIC NATURE OF THE SCENE,
THE SENSE OF MOVEMENT OF
THE COMPOSITION IS QUITE
MARKED.

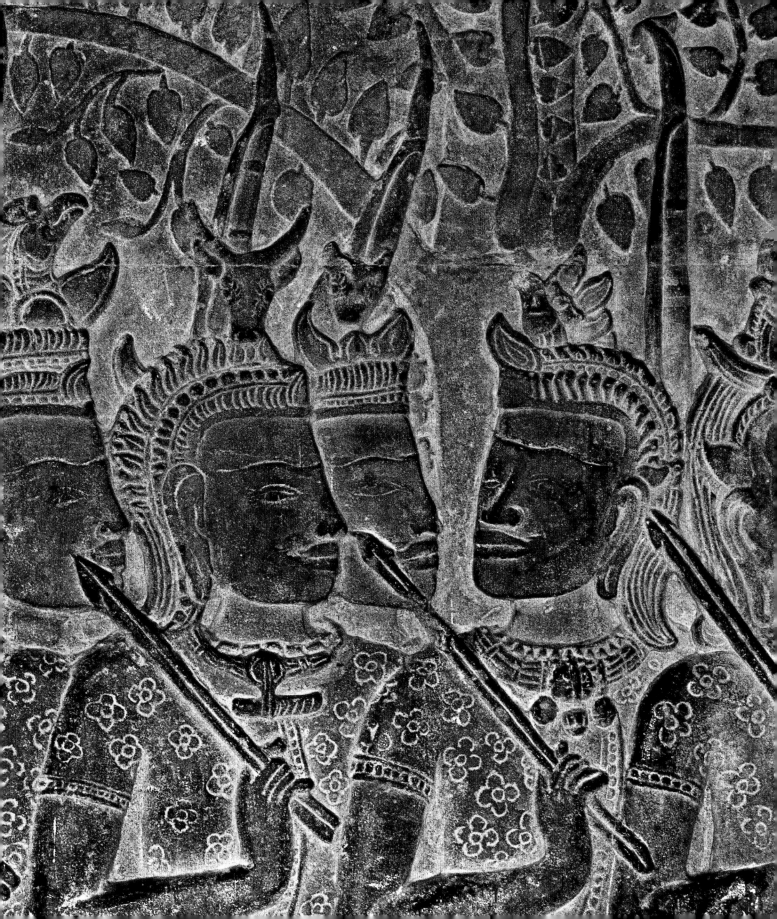

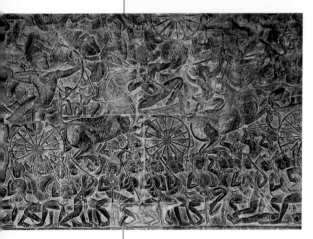

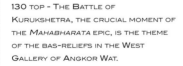

**130** TOP - THE BATTLE OF
KURUKSHETRA, THE CRUCIAL MOMENT OF
THE *Mahabharata* EPIC, IS THE THEME
OF THE BAS-RELIEFS IN THE WEST
GALLERY OF ANGKOR WAT.

**130** BOTTOM - THE CYCLE OF BAS-RELIEFS
THAT NARRATES THE STRUGGLE BETWEEN
THE TWO RIVAL AND RELATED CLANS, THE
PANDAVA AND KAURAVA, ACTUALLY
DEPICTS THE KHMER ARMY WITH ITS GAMUT
OF SOLDIERS AND EQUIPMENT.

130-131 - Sinners being led to hell. The drama of this scene is heightened by the hierarchy, both human and moral, represented by the size of the figures.

131 top - Ferocious animals devour those who have not obeyed the code of moral conduct, who are being judged by Yama.

131 bottom - The cruel representation of the punishment meted out to sinners plays an important role in the Judgment of the Dead reliefs.

132-133 - THE 21 DIVINITIES IN THE ANCIENT VEDIC PANTHEON AND THEIR ARMY FIGHT AT CLOSE QUARTERS AGAINST THE DEMONS DURING THE BATTLE OF LANKA.

133 - A SCENE FROM THE BATTLE OF KURUKSHETRA: THE POSITIONS OF THE FIGURES, MUCH LIKE A DANCE, MAY INDEED HAVE BEEN INSPIRED BY CHOREOGRAPHIC PERFORMANCES.

134-135 - ROWS OF HEROES OF THE *MAHABHARATA* WITH SHIELDS ARE LINED UP IN THE BAS-RELIEFS THAT DECORATE THE INNER GALLERY OF THE BAYON.

Another feature of Angkor Wat is the 1,876 celestial nymphs (*apsaras*) scattered here and there throughout the complex, with clothing and accessories that afford a perfect image of the various types of women in the king's court: concubines, dancers, servants, etc. Like the myriad other images that cover the entire monument and are in different states of preservation, these nymphs are sometimes barely perceptible because of the fine and subtle carving.

Despite the many studies and the constant research made, Angkor Wat still has unsolved mysteries, including the very sense of its existence. The fact that it is now a Buddhist temple and has been for five hundred years merely explains its prestige, which has remained unchanged over the cen-

turies. Its orientation to the West can be explained by its being dedicated to Vishnu, who is associated with this cardinal point, as well as by the fact that this is the direction of the setting sun and of death. The latter observation has led scholars to think that the grandiose complex was built as an immense mausoleum for Suryavarman II that would house his ashes and preserve his memory. There are also other interpretations of this monument—astronomical, astrological, cosmological and, obviously, religious—that, as amply demonstrated for most of temples in India, which were a constant and primary source of inspiration for the Khmer, would explain the layout of the structure as well the precision and solidity of its construction.

138 LEFT AND 139 RIGHT –
THE TRANSFORMATION FROM
CELESTIAL NYMPHS TO
COURTESANS TAKES PLACE BY
MEANS OF THE PHYSICAL
FEATURES AND POSES, AND
TOP ALL BY THE RENDERING OF
THE SUMPTUOUS ORNAMENTS
AND ELABORATE HAIR STYLES.

138-139 – THE ROWS OF
APSARAS AT ANGKOR WAT
CODIFIED AN IDEAL OF FEMALE
BEAUTY THAT LASTED FOR
CENTURIES IN THE KHMER
MILIEU.

140 AND 141 - THE INTRODUCTION OF THE
APSARA (AT LEFT, DETAIL OF AN APSARA
WITH A FINELY WROUGHT BELT AND
BRACELET; AT RIGHT, THE UPPER PART OF
THE SAME FIGURE, HIGHLIGHTING THE
EXTREMELY ELABORATE HAIR STYLE) IN A
DECORATIVE CONTEXT TENDS TO BRING
THE HUMAN WORLD CLOSER TO THE
NATURAL ONE AND LINKS BOTH TO A
DIVINE IDEAL.

The ancient Khmer sculptors' ability in carving stone was party inherited from India, but soon evolved into a highly original local style that in turn greatly influenced all Southeast Asian art. Most of Khmer sculpture is in stone, and this explains the huge amount of finds in our possession (although an even greater quantity was probably destroyed or pillaged). The subjects are for the most part Hindu divinities, predominantly Vishnu the preserver and Shiva the destroyer, Brahma the preserver, the elephant-headed god Ganesha (the protector of commerce), female divinities, and many other figures in the rich Hindu pantheon. There are also creatures with an animal likeness or fantastic beings, all derived from ancient Indian mythology: the serpent Naga, the demon Kala, the gigantic crocodile-dragon Makara, and the lions. Some large sculptures, or sculpture cycles, drew inspiration from the crucial passages in the *Mahabharata* and *Ramayana* epics or from legends of "ancient history" handed down in the *Purana*, as well as in the treatises regarding various sciences or arts, the *Shastra*. Far from being mere provincial art in the immense territory of the Indian sphere of influence, Khmer art not only has original features but also a superhuman dimension that is able to condense and synthesize the multiplicity and limitations of artistic experience into a grandiose and immutable cosmic reality.

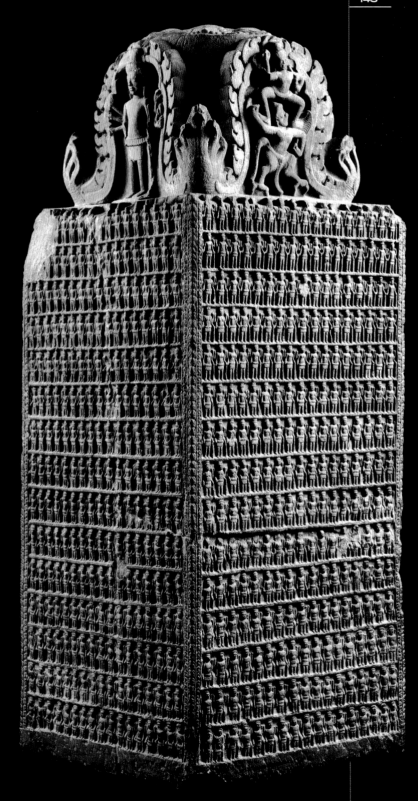

142 - THIS GUARDIAN LION FROM LOPBURI (H. 57 IN.) IS DISTINGUISHED BY ITS HIGHLY DEFINED DETAILS (NATIONAL MUSEUM, BANGKOK).

143 LEFT - A BAPHUON STYLE HEAD OF A DIVINITY (H. 7.5 IN.) REMARKABLE FOR ITS HEIGHTENED REALISM (MUSÉE GUIMET, PARIS).

143 RIGHT - THIS VISHNUITE RELIQUARY (H. 54 IN.) FOUND IN THE PREAH KHAN COMPLEX PROVIDES AN INTERESTING EXAMPLE OF THE ANGKOR WAT STYLE, CHARACTERIZED BY THE DIMENSIONALITY AND SYMMETRY OF THE FIGURES (MUSÉE GUIMET, PARIGI).

144 - PROTECTED BY A *NAGA*
DURING HIS MEDITATION, THIS
11TH-CENTURY BUDDHA (H.
40.5 IN.) IS DISTINGUISHED
BY THE STUDIED SIMPLICITY
OF THE COMPOSITION
(MUSÉE GUIMET).

145 - THE INTENSE
CONCENTRATION AND
NOBILITY OF BUDDHA ARE
HIGHLIGHTED IN WHAT
REMAINS OF THIS
SCULPTURE A FINE EXAMPLE
OF KHMER ART (PRIVATE
COLLECTION).

In a later period Buddhist iconography flanked Hindu motifs. The sculpture dedicated to the Enlightened One attained the apogee of perfection in the Bayon of Angkor Thom, where magnificent portraits of the bodhisattva Avalokiteshvara and of Buddha were carved on about fifty towers, each with four faces. The rapid development of portraits of the bodhisattvas and so many other Buddhist personages (who in turn acquired almost divine characteristics that were quite remote from the original concept of this religion) side by side with the main Hindu divinities produced important results. It prevented a traumatic rupture in the iconography of the two religions, and also led to the interaction and exchange of features, and even to the coexistence of the two iconographies, both in daily cult worship and in artistic representation. Many people point out that Khmer art contains a basic hieratic quality and excessive stereotypy. This is partly true (and is justified by the almost immutable stylistic features over the centuries, which in Oriental art is regarded as a virtue), but should not be considered an absolute fact. Despite the fact that each sculpture has the salient features of the person portrayed in keeping with the descriptions in the mythological texts and treatises, the sculptors had a certain amount of creative freedom in rendering the details. One instance of this are the stone sculptures of the *apsaras* (celestial nymphs) at Angkor Wat, each of which has a different posture and varying decoration and ornaments.

At the same time, the idea of an art exclusively given over to religious or mythological purposes is either mistaken or partial. In fact, there is no lack of works with secular themes. Cycles of bas-reliefs, such as those at Angkor Thom, depict important events in the history of the empire, such as the wars against the Cham or other foreign invaders, and relate the daily life of the Khmer with great attention paid to detail and with astonishing narrative skill.

146 - A STATUE OF THE
BODHISATTVA VAJRAPANI
(H. 42 IN.) THAT IS BOTH
TERRIFYING AND BENEVOLENT.
FROM THE END OF THE 10TH
CENTURY ON, BUDDHIST
ICONOGRAPHY BECAME MORE
AND MORE IMPORTANT AND
FINALLY PREVAILED (MUSÉE
GUIMET, PARIS).

147 - HEAD OF BUDDHA
(H. 15 IN.) WITH TYPICAL
KHMER FEATURES AND THE
THICK CURLY HAIR THAT MARKS
THE PREVAILING STYLE IN THE
11TH CENTURY (MUSÉE
GUIMET, PARIS).

148 - A BRONZE PORTRAIT
OF LOKESHVARA (H. 17 IN.)
THAT LINKS PRINCELY ATTIRE
AND ORNAMENTS TO THE
BUDDHIST ATTRIBUTES,
INCLUDING THE HANDS IN
VARIOUS *MUDRA* RITUAL
GESTURES (NATIONAL
MUSEUM, PHNOM PENH).

149 - THIS LATE 12TH-
CENTURY BRONZE STATUE IS
A RARE REPRESENTATION OF
SADASHIVA (H. 13 IN.), THAT
IS, SHIVA IN THE GUISE OF
THE SUPREME LORD
(NATIONAL MUSEUM,
PHNOM PENH).

150 bottom - This gilded
bronze sculpture of the
seated Buddha flanked by
two bodhisattvas
expresses the profundity
of the doctrine
associated with his
manifold manifestation
(Private Collection).

150-151 - The remains of a
bronze statue of Vishnu
resting after creating
the universe (h. 48 in.)
were found in the West
Mebon (National
Museum, Phnom Penh).

It is sad to think that after the death of such a splendid king as Suryavarman II, the empire was overrun with palace conspiracies and behind-the-scenes struggles for power, but it is certainly not surprising. This ruler was probably succeeded by a usurper, Yashovarman II, who was then assassinated by a court official in 1165. Several years had to pass before a great personage such as Jayavarman VII would restore prestige to an empire that seemed to have lost all capability to control the numerous kingdoms and potentates that in fact were the very fabric of the empire.

Suryavarman II consolidated the structures and territory of the empire, while Jayavarman VII (1181-1220) provided further stone edifices and splendid works of art. One of the greatest Khmer rulers, he ordered the construction of the impressive Buddhist structures at Bayon and Angkor Thom as part of an enterprising building program that was in fact the vastest in the long dynastic history of the Khmer empire, also producing important public works such as roads, bridges, and rest houses along the main communication routes. A devout Mahayana Buddhist, Jayavar-

man VII instilled this doctrine of the Enlightened One into every aspect of Khmer life.

However, this period began inauspiciously. In fact, in 1177, before Jayavarman VII could effectively take power, a brilliantly planned and executed naval expedition on the part of the Cham, led by their king Jaya Indravarman, skirted southern Vietnam, went up the Mekong Delta and the Tonlé Sap River and then penetrated the Great Lake. From here the Cham reached Angkor, which they sacked and set on fire. This disastrous defeat, the worst in Khmer history up to that time, led to a brief period of Cham dominion, which ended four years later, when Jayavarman VII, already fifty years old, led the Khmer in the reconquest of the city through a land and naval battle that made the Great Lake red with blood. He made Angkor the capital for forty years. However, this victory was not enough to cancel such a humiliating defeat. Consequently, in 1190 the Khmer army invaded Champa and brought the Cham king back to Angkor in chains. The successive annexation of Champa in 1203 was short-lived, as it lasted only until the king's death in 1220.

152 - JAYAVARMAN VII, PORTRAYED HERE IN SANDSTONE (H. 16 IN.), WAS THE LAST OF THE GREAT KHMER RULERS AND DID MUCH BUILDING AT ANGKOR THOM (NATIONAL MUSEUM, PHNOM PENH).

153 - ACCORDING TO THE MOST PLAUSIBLE AND ACKNOWLEDGED THEORY, THIS STATUE (H. 49 IN.) REPRESENTS JAYARAJADEVI ("THE GODDESS OF THE VICTORIOUS KING"), THE FIRST WIFE OF JAYAVARMAN VII (MUSÉE GUIMET, PARIS).

In many respects Jayavarman was the greatest Khmer sovereign, and he was undoubtedly a great builder. He set up his residence in an urban area of the capital (which in our time would be called "upgraded") that was called Angkor Thom ("Great City"), a true city within a city measuring three kilometers per side and surrounded by a moat and tall walls made of laterite. Here the king restored the original sumptuousness of the old royal palace and the surrounding edifices; opposite them, to the east, he built the Elephant Terrace and the Terrace of the Leper King, which was probably the cremation site consecrated to the god of death, Yama, who is depicted in the famous "Leper King" statue that dominates it.

Angkor Thom has five entrances (two on the east side), each one with a double portal flanked by stone elephants. Surmount-

154-155 - ENORMOUS
FOUR-HEADED SCULPTURES
DOMINATE THE IMPRESSIVE
GOPURA (H. 75.5 FT) OF THE
SOUTH GATE OF ANGKOR
THOM, THE CAPITAL CITY OF
JAYAVARMAN VII.

155 - THE NORTH GATE OF
ANGKOR THOM IS NORMALLY
USED AS AN EXIT BY VISITORS.
THREE-HEADED ELEPHANTS
TOWERED OVER BY THE FIGURE
OF THE GOD INDRA SUPPORT
THE STRUCTURE AT THE SIDES.

In the center of this urban complex is the Bayon, Jayavarman VII's state temple. Although it was dedicated to the Mahayana Buddhist cult, this complex abounds in images of Hindu divinities. Except for the view of Angkor Wat at sunset, nothing moves visitors so much as the four-headed *bodhisattva* of compassion, Avalokiteshvara, that is reproduced no fewer than 54 times on the towers of the temple and faces the four cardinal points. These images are both remote and intense and may very well bear the stylized facial features of the king who, in conformity with his Buddhist faith, had refused the title of *chakravartin* (Universal Ruler) but not his dreams of grandeur and immortality. Similar features are to be found on the statue found at Preah Khan, which according to tradition portrays the king meditating. The vast and long sequences of bas-relief cycles in the interior of the complex may not have the same artistic value as those in Angkor Wat, but the representations of the great battle against the Cham to reconquer Angkor, and the detailed depictions of everyday and court life, are invaluable sources of documentary

ing the entrances are five large heads of Buddha (four of which face the cardinal points and one, once covered with gold leaf, in the middle). Beyond the walls the complex is bounded by a large moat crossed over by impressive stone causeways. On either side of this passageway are 54 statues of *devas* (gods) and *asuras* (demons), depicted as formidable warriors with a menacing air who grasp the stone balustrades carved in the form of *nagas*.

information. To this must be added the testimony of Zhou Daguan, a member of the diplomatic mission of the Chinese Empire during the Yuan Dynasty (of Mongolian origin). Zhou lived at Angkor from 1296 to 1297, and upon his return he wrote *Notes on the Customs of Cambodia*. His account is not always first-hand and has been preserved only partially, but in any case it contains a great deal of precious information.

156 TOP - HEADS OF *ASURAS* FLANK THE ACCESS TO THE NORTH GATE OF THE CITY OF ANGKOR THOM.

156 CENTER - THE PARADE OF GIANTS ENDS WITH THE TIP OF THE *NAGA*.

156 BOTTOM - THE GIANTS WERE MADE OF BLOCKS OF STONE SCULPTED ONE BY ONE AND THEN LAID OVER ONE ANOTHER.

156-157 - THE BALUSTRADE OF THE *NAGA* SUPPORTED BY 54 SUPERNATURAL BEINGS (AT RIGHT, GODS; AT LEFT, DEMONS) EXTENDS ALONG THE AVENUE THAT AFFORDS ACCESS TO NORTH GATE OF ANGKOR THOM: THE PARADE REFERS TO THE CHURNING OF THE OCEAN OF MILK AND THE CREATION.

158 - THE TERRACE OF THE ELEPHANTS, OVERLOOKING A MILITARY AVENUE, IS ONE OF THE ATTRACTIONS IN ANGKOR THOM. HERE WE SEE ONE OF THE FIGURES THAT IDEALLY SUPPORTS THE TERRACE.

159 TOP LEFT - THE CONSTRUCTIONS OVER THE TERRACE OF THE ELEPHANTS, USED FOR CEREMONIES, HAD PARTS MADE OF WOOD THAT NO LONGER EXIST.

159 TOP RIGHT - THE CENTRAL STAIRWAY IS DECORATED WITH LIONS AND GARUDAS. THE TERRACE OF THE ELEPHANTS IS MADE UP OF THREE DISTINCT SECTIONS THAT TOGETHER ARE 984 FEET LONG.

159 BOTTOM LEFT - THE FIVE-HEADED HORSE AT THE NORTHERN END OF THE TERRACE OF THE ELEPHANTS IS SURROUNDED BY APSARAS AND ARMED DEMONS CHASING OTHER FIGURES.

159 BOTTOM RIGHT - REPRESENTATIONS OF PACHYDERMS STAND OUT ON THE FAÇADE OF THE TERRACE OF THE ELEPHANTS. THESE ALMOST LIFE-SIZE IMAGES ABOUND IN INTERESTING DETAILS.

160-161 - THE TERRACE OF THE ELEPHANTS, SET ON THE EAST OF THE WALLS OF ANGKOR THOM, WAS SO NAMED BECAUSE OF THE REPRESENTATIONS OF THESE ANIMALS AND THE RIDERS.

162 TOP - DETAIL OF A SECTION OF THE GALLERIES OF BAS-RELIEF SCULPTURE THAT DECORATE THE TERRACE OF THE LEPER KING, LAID OUT ON SEVEN SUPERPOSED REGISTERS.

162 BOTTOM - THE LEPER KING, A PROBABLE REPRESENTATION OF THE GOD OF THE DEAD YAMA, WAS ORIGINALLY PLACED ON THE TERRACE NAMED AFTER HIM (NATIONAL MUSEUM, PHNOM PENH).

162-163 - THE TERRACE OF THE LEPER KING, MEASURING 82 FEET PER SIDE AND 20 FEET HIGH, IS RICHLY DECORATED WITH MYTHOLOGICAL BEINGS AND FEMALE FIGURES.

164-165 - THE ROYAL PALACE AT ANGKOR THOM ("GREAT CITY") IS THE CENTER OF WHAT WAS THE LAST CAPITAL OF THE ANGKOR REGION (LATE 12TH-EARLY 13TH CENTURY).

166-167 - THE BAYON, BUILT AT DIFFERENT TIMES AND SET OVER A MORE ANCIENT STRUCTURE, IS ONE OF THE MAJOR FEATURES OF ANGKOR THOM.

167 TOP AND BOTTOM LEFT - THE ENTRANCE TO THE ROYAL PALACE AREA AT ANGKOR THOM IS MARKED BY SOME STONE GOPURAS, WHILE THE RESIDENTIAL BUILDINGS HAVE DISAPPEARED BECAUSE THEY WERE MADE OF WOOD.

167 BOTTOM RIGHT - THE ARCHITECTURAL COMPLEXITY AND ORIGINALITY OF THE BAYON ARE HIGHLIGHTED IN THIS VIEW FROM THE NORTHEASTERN SIDE OF THE TEMPLE BUILT BY JAYAVARMAN VII.

**168** TOP - UNLIKE THE FIRST LEVEL OF THE BAYON, WHICH WAS OPEN TO ALL CITIZENS AND WAS USED FOR BOTH CIVIL AND CEREMONIAL PURPOSES, THE SECOND AND THIRD WERE USED ONLY FOR CULT RITUALS.

**168** BOTTOM - ONE OF THE CORNER TOWERS OVERLOOKING THE INNER GALLERY OF THE BAYON.

**169** - THE PORTRAIT OF THE BODHISATTVA AVALOKITESHVARA—WHICH IS PROBABLY REALLY A LIKENESS OF JAYAVARMAN VIII —IS REPEATED OBSESSIVELY IN THE BAYON, A CENTER OF THE BUDDHIST CULT.

While the description of the Chinese diplomat is of absolute value in solving many of the doubts that concerning the history of the Khmer, most of what we know concerning the daily life of this civilization (which is not much, however, compared to other cultures) comes from the splendid bas-reliefs that decorated the walls of some temples at Angkor, especially those at Angkor Wat and the Bayon. These long and, on the whole, well preserved cycles give us an idea of

aspects of Khmer daily life, but provides no information regarding the reality of court life, which was off-limits to foreigners. For example, Zhou describes the characteristics of the inhabitants: medium height, black curly hair, rather square faces and broad foreheads, straight noses with large nostrils, and deep-set eyes. All these features are not dissimilar from those of the modern-day Cambodians, and the clothes are also to some degree the same, at least the practical *sampot*, a

these people's clothing, work activities and even food. Moreover, the sculptures depict the domestic animals, means of transportation, houses, and flora and fauna that were an integral part of the Khmers' existence. What strikes one most is the similarity with rural life in present-day Cambodia, while the physical features of the dominating class and the kings are still partly wrapped in mystery, since it is difficult to understand whether the representations were realistic or conformed to a sort of ritual abstraction. However, there is a direct source that historians have drawn from liberally, partly because of its liveliness and partly because of the accuracy of the data it furnishes: once again, the travel journal of Zhou Daguan.

His account, which is quite detailed, covers practically all

rectangular band of cloth worn by both men and women but draped in a different manner. The striking difference in the apparel of the commoners and nobles lay in the value of the cloth (silk imported from China or Siam instead of cotton) and its decoration (the king's clothing had gold threads woven into elaborate patterns). The lunar cycles, which affected the rice harvest and the ebb and flow of the waters of the Great Lake (Tonlé Sap), were the chronological horizon in which the life of the Khmer took place, accompanied by feast days, some of which—especially those connected to the full moon—are still celebrated.

Obviously all this was endured rather than lived by the social class that contributed more than any other to the greatness of Khmer empire—the numerous slaves. This class was

made up of persons who had fallen into debt, petty and middle-range criminals, prisoners of war, and members of minority ethnic groups. These people were at the bottom of the social scale, at the apex of which were the nobles and priests, while the warriors and farmers formed the largest classes. The role of women seems to have been important, as they had leading political and economic posts, in keeping with the traditional matrilineal descent of the Khmer rulers.

170 AND 170-171 - THE BAS-RELIEF WORKS THAT DECORATE THE WALL OF THE OUTER GALLERY IN THE BAYON DEPICT, AMONG THE MANY SCENES, A MILITARY PARADE WITH ELEPHANTS AND CHARIOTS CONNECTED TO THE BATTLE BETWEEN THE KHMER AND CHAM. THIS SCENE OCCUPIES A LONG PANEL LAID OUT ON SEVERAL REGISTERS AND FRAMES ONE OF THE ENTRANCES TO THE SECOND LEVEL OF THE TEMPLE.

171 BOTTOM - TWO ROWS OF PILLARS WITH A SQUARE PLINTH SUPPORTED THE ROOF OF THE OUTER GALLERY OF THE BAYON, ON THE BACK WALL OF WHICH THE KHMER ARTISTS SCULPTED A LONG SERIES OF RELIEF WORK.

Northeast of Angkor Thom, the reservoir built by Jayavarman, the Jayatataka baray (the "Sea of Victory") is "only" 2 miles long and half a mile wide, therefore much smaller than the immense West Baray and East Baray (and here again arises the question of the true purpose of these huge artificial lakes) but is beautified by its temple island, the Neak Pean, dedicated to the bodhisattva Avalokiteshvara.

Jayavarman VII seems to have been particularly interested in the health of his subjects, given the construction of 102 hospitals throughout the empire and of pools and hot springs that were used by pilgrims visiting the Neak Pean. Much smaller than the Jayatataka, the Srah Srang pond is situated south of the East Baray. It seems that the king was especially fond of this sort of "royal bath," which already existed before his time but to which Jayavarman added majestic access stairways. This is a site that is indeed special, especially at sunset, which can be viewed from the platform facing West that is dominated by lions and *nagas* and that offers a breathtaking spectacle.

While in preceding works—leaving aside their intrinsic value, which makes many of them unique and fundamental in the history of Khmer civilization—Jayavarman VII continued consolidated civil and religious architectural traditions, and the construction of the citadel-monasteries was truly an innovation.

This king, a fervent Buddhist, gave to the monastic community—of which he was naturally the patron—three residential and religious complexes surrounded by moats and walls, each quite beautiful and with different features. The largest of these (and also the most heterogeneous, both as a building type and in its religious inspiration and iconography, once again a combination of Buddhism and Hinduism, as well as of the dynastic cult) is Preah Khan, just west of the Jayatataka. What some scholars feel was a study center more than a true monastery— in any case, used to house 15,000 residents—was built on the site of the famous battle against the Cham with the aid of 97,840 inhabitants of the surrounding villages (as detailed chronicles relate).

172 top - The rich symbolism of Neak Pean makes this small Buddhist sanctuary a very important monument.

172 bottom - The horse Balaha, which was once immersed in the reservoir water, is represented while swimming to save the hapless victims of a shipwreck in a Buddhist legend concerning Avalokiteshvara, of whom it is the manifestation.

172-173 - THE PREAH KHAN, OR "SACRED
SWORD," ON THE BANK OF THE JAYATATAKA
BARAY, AT THE NORTHERN TIP OF ANGKOR,
IS LIKE TA PROHM IN A STATE OF SEMI-
ABANDONMENT, COVERED WITH VEGETATION.

173 BOTTOM - THE ACCESS PORTAL OF
PREAH KHAN. THIS BUDDHIST COMPLEX
ALSO HAS WELL DEFINED AREAS
CONSECRATED TO THE VISHNU, SHIVA
AND ANCESTOR CULTS.

174-175 - In the northern section of the Preah Khan complex, the image of the ascetic Shiva that is repeated in a sculpted register at the base of the monuments.

174 bottom - *Apsaras* in the vivacious, almost caricatural Bayon style adorn the Pavilion of the Dancers, the first structure one comes upon when entering from the east (and main) entrance of Preah Khan.

175 top - The columned two-story edifice in the Preah Khan enclosure may have housed the 'sacred sword' that symbolized royal power, after which the complex was named.

175

175 center - This gallery overlooks the first court in Preah Khan, a vast complex that could house thousands of monks and pilgrims and whose many buildings had different functions.

175 bottom - The walls enclosing the second court of Preah Khan are decorated with niches containing figures of divinities and surfaces sculpted in relief with plant motifs.

176 TOP - *NAGA* SERPENTS DECORATE THE
AVENUES OF PREAH KHAN, WHICH WAS
NOT ONLY DAMAGED BY NATURE BUT ALSO
SUFFERED THE DESTRUCTIVE FURY OF THE
BRAHMINS IN THE 13TH CENTURY.

176 CENTER - THE STRUCTURAL AND
IDEAL CENTER OF PREAH KHAN, THIS
16TH-CENTURY *STUPA* REPLACED A
STATUE OF LOKESHVARA IN THE GUISE OF
THE FATHER OF JAYAVARMAN VII.

176 BOTTOM - THE INTERIOR OF THE
CENTRAL SANCTUARY IN PREAH KHAN IS
CHARACTERIZED BY ITS EXTREME
SIMPLICITY AND TYPICAL KHMER
ARCHITECTURE, WHICH NEVER USE ARCHES.

176-177 - THE WEST ENTRANCE TO THE
PREAH KHAN COMPLEX WAS PRECEDED
BY TWO STATUES OF GUARDIANS, WHILE
TOP THE GATE IS A REPRESENTATION OF
THE BATTLE OF LANKA.

The second of these innovative structures in size, but much more famous because of the dramatic coexistence of nature and human works, is the Ta Prohm. The École Française d'Extrême Orient (EFEO) restored this site to a limited degree in order to safeguard the stability of some edifices while at the same making some parts of the citadel accessible. An inscription states that 12,640 monks-workmen were used to build this site (perhaps the same persons who were to live there), with the help of around 80,000 inhabitants in the vicinity. This was an immense work, if we take into account the technical difficulties involved and the problems of furnishing building materials such as stone, which were not available in large quantities on the site. But today the sight of these ancient edifices enveloped and often strangled by the roots of gigantic trees–figs, banyan and silk cotton–and somewhat disfigured by the moss, again connects the

grandeur of Angkor to Man's ancient dream of immortality, which is above all the illusion of being able to dominate nature and its elements, as well as to a more personal and evocative level. It is no accident that Ta Prohm is one of the most popular sights at Angkor, despite the fact that from a purely artistic or urbanistic standpoint it has nothing new to offer, except perhaps its two-fold function as a place of worship and a monastery.

178 TOP - THERE ARE MANY ARCHITECTURAL ELEMENTS IN RUINS LYING IN THE INNER COURT OF TA PROHM, WHILE THE SIDE GALLERIES ARE OVERGROWN WITH VEGETATION.

178 BOTTOM - ELABORATE TOWERS DOMINATE THE INNER SECTION OF THE TA PROHM.

178-179 - A MONUMENTAL ACCESS INTRODUCES VISITORS TO TA PROHM, THE SECOND OF THE BUDDHIST COMPLEXES BUILT FOR JAYAVARMAN VII.

180-181 - THE SHEER SIZE OF TA PROHM MAKES ONE FEEL ALMOST CLAUSTROPHOBIC, A SENSATION ACCENTUATED BY THE TREES THAT SEEM TO BE SUFFOCATING THE GALLERIES.

182 top and 182-183 - *Apsaras* placed in niches alternate with Buddhist religious motifs on the walls in the inner section of the Ta Prohm complex.

182 bottom - The gallery with a corbelled vault is situated in the third court of the sacred complex of Ta Prohm.

The third and last of these complexes is quite a different matter, because it was inhabited by religious communities almost continuously until the 1960s and is much smaller. This is the Banteay Kdei ("The Citadel of the Cells"), which overlooks the west bank of the Srah Srang. In a poor state of preservation, partly because of the low-quality sandstone used in its construction, its similarity to Ta Prohm (despite its smaller size) is accentuated by the presence of four *gopuras*, each with four stone faces oriented to the cardinal points, and of representations of *garudas*.

184 TOP - A LION AND A *NAGA* GUARD THE SACRED AREA OF BANTEAY KDEI.

184 CENTER - THE HALL OF THE DANCERS IN THE BANTEAY KDEI COMPLEX IS DISTINGUISHED FOR THE PILLARS DECORATED WITH FIGURES OF *APSARAS*.

184 BOTTOM - THE FOUR-HEADED IMAGE OF THE BODHISATTVA AVALOKITESHVARA DOMINATES THE BANTEAY KDEI ("CITADEL OF THE CELLS"), THE THIRD COMPLEX BUILT BY THE ZEALOUS KING JAYAVARMAN VII.

184-185 - THE *GOPURA* ALLOWS ONE TO GO PAST THE SECOND ENCLOSURE WALL OF BANTEAY KDEI AND ENTER ITS CENTRAL AREA.

186 - Some *apsaras* between the friezes of the Terrace of the Dancers in the Banteay Kdei complex.

187 top - Structural weaknesses and the use of rather perishable material such as laterite were partly responsible for the deterioration of Banteay Kdei,

which is represented here by a view of the Hall of the Dancers, an edifice that lies east of the central sanctuary.

187 bottom - Statues of *apsaras* and panels alternate along the inner walls of the enclosure that includes the central sanctuary of Banteay Kdei.

Naturally, among the many works commissioned by this extraordinary figure were other localities lying quite a distance from the Khmer power center but still connected to Angkor by a road network that was enlarged and improved by this ruler through the construction of bridges and rest houses, which were certainly indispensable for the management of an empire that took in almost all continental Southeast Asia. The largest of these localities, as well as the most mysterious in many respects, is Banteay Chhmar, the "Narrow Fortress," located in the jungles near the northwest Cambodia-Thailand border. The city, 93 miles from Angkor, was probably already important during the reign of Jayavarman II. And while it did not equal the splendor of the capital, it was of great strategic importance for control of the western and northern provinces, which are now part of Thailand. Jayavarman VII beautified and enlarged the complex, dedicating it to his son who died while fighting against the Cham, and to the four military commanders who were also killed while defending the capital during the 1177 invasion. Surrounded by other temples, the structures in this complex immediately strike one for their similarity to the architecture of Angkor Wat and Angkor Thom. It is enclosed by walls and by a broad moat, and the enclosure has a surface area of 3.5 square miles. Besides the outstanding, albeit rather dilapidated, architecture, Banteay Chhmar is famous for the bas-reliefs that provide such a lively and detailed representation of the battle against the Cham, as well as other scenes drawn from Hindu mythology or from Buddhist hagiographic tradition. The rep-

resentations of kut (the traditional Indian garudas) were dedicated to the protection of the temple, which was a way of emphasizing the glory of the king. Original features at Banteay Chhmar, because they are not to be found in other complexes, are the images of kinnari, legendary winged creatures with a woman's body. From an artistic standpoint Banteay Chhmar stands out for the bas-relief sculpture depicting the figure of Avalokiteshvara with several pairs of arms, and those representing scenes of court life. Similar to Bayon in its architecture, Banteay Chhmar differs in the type of decoration, including the sculpture work on the lintels with the Buddha Vairocana, who has four heads and eight ears, the 32-arm Avalokiteshvara, a central figure in Mahayana Buddhism, and, on the east wall, yet another depiction of the terrible battle against the Cham, a central element in the creation of Banteay Chhmar, whose destination as a shrine to Prince Sintravarman and the faithful generals who died in battle is questionable.

This is a truly vast complex (according to the French archaeologist George Groslier, who drew up a partial map of it in the 1930s, it may be even larger than Angkor Wat), but for reasons that are partly unknown (including the recent pillaging by thieves in search of ancient treasures for the international market) it also has a very chaotic plan and is in a very poor state of preservation. Its main function was supposedly to house the remains of a highborn and high-ranking prince, but this theory hardly fits in with other elements such as the vast baray (1 mile long) with an island temple in the middle that Groslier himself found to the east of the temple complex.

188 LEFT - BANTEAY CHHMAR IS ONE OF THE LEAST KNOWN AND MOST DAMAGED KHMER SITES, AS CAN BE SEEN IN THIS DOOR WITH SCULPTED DECORATION.

188 RIGHT - SCULPTED DEPICTIONS OF AVALOKITESVARA DECORATE THESE JAMBS IN THE BANTEAY CHHMAR COMPLEX, NEAR THE CAMBODIA-THAILAND BORDER.

189 - BANTEAY CHHMAR, WHOSE MOST IMMEDIATE INSPIRATION WAS ANGKOR THOM, WAS DEDICATED TO AVALOKITESVARA, WHO IS PORTRAYED ON THE TOP SECTION OF THE TOWERS. THIS COMPLEX HARKS BACK TO THE ANCIENT GRANDEUR OF THE KHMER, WHICH WAS REVIVED BY JAYAVARMAN VII, WHO DEDICATED THE MAIN TEMPLE TO HIS SON WHO HAD DIED IN BATTLE.

190-191 - ORIGINAL
DEPICTIONS OF
AVOKITESVARA WITH 32 ARMS
STAND OUT ON THE WALLS OF
BANTEAY CHHMAR.

191 - THE PRINCIPAL
SCULPTURE CYCLES IN THE
BANTEAY CHHMAR
COMPLEX, WHICH WERE
EXECUTED AT THE BEHEST
OF JAYAVARMAN VII, AN
EXCEPTIONAL MILITARY CHIEF
AS WELL AS ADMINISTRATOR,

BEAR WITNESS TO BOTH THE
STRUGGLES THE KHMER
EMPIRE CARRIED OUT TO
ATTAIN ITS SPLENDOR AND
ITS HIGH LEVEL OF CULTURE.

192-193 - THE ANCIENT
ENEMIES OF THE KHMER,
THE CHAM, SEEN IN THIS
BAS-RELIEF AT ANGKOR WAT,
TOOK ADVANTAGE OF THE
DEATH OF JAYAVARMAN VII,
WHICH LED TO THE CRISIS
OF KHMER POWER

## SPLENDOR AND CRISIS

The death of Jayavarman VII, which occurred around the year 1215, ended the apogee of the Khmer. Their empire, which had been extended up to the border with the kingdom of Pagan, in Burma, took in part of Laos and almost all the Malaysian peninsula, and was so well organized and administrated it seemed destined to crown the dreams of eternity of the *chakravartin*, the semi-divine universal rulers. But obviously this was not to be. It was certainly the case for at least a century, under the successors of Jayavarman VII (Indravarman II and Jayavarman VIII). In fact, Chinese sources speak of a flourishing capital with an abundance of outstanding monuments in the middle of a Cambodia that wayfarers coming even from distant lands considered "rich and noble." These merchants, who had made such difficult and fatiguing journeys, were eager to take advantage of the security and services offered by the Khmer empire, and as they were simply overwhelmed by the amazing structures that towered over the plain and were reflected in reservoirs that were as large as lakes, might have failed to notice the difficulties there. At the end of the 13th century a temporary revival of Hinduism as the state religion and the persecution of Buddhism may have sparked one of the least known and most tragic events in the history of Khmer civilization: the destruction of Buddhist images. This was veritable iconoclastic fury, if it is true that all the statues of Buddha at Angkor were mutilated, including the large effigy of the seated Enlightened One in the central shrine of the Bayon, and that none of the 45,000 images that decorated the top of the walls of Preah Khan, Ta Prohm and Banteay Kdei remained standing. Thousands of statues were smashed to pieces and the fragments buried deep in the ground. Such Buddhist-inspired sites as the Bayon and Angkor Wat were adapted to Hindu worship, as were other minor edifices. The perpetrators of, and the reasons behind, this destruction and partial conversion of images and architecture to Hindu worship are still unknown—just as we know nothing concerning the consequences this furious wave of persecution had on the Buddhist clergy and community. But what was certainly a manifestation of religious intolerance that was both unprecedented and with few sequels in Asia, can most probably be dated to the reign of Jayavarman VIII. Be that as it may, the time of Mahayana had passed. Under Indravarman III (1295-1307), in fact, Theravada Buddhism (the so-called Lesser Vehicle, the form that aimed at restoring the doctrinal rigor of early Buddhism), which was spread throughout Southeast Asia by missionary monks from Sri Lanka, now also took root among the Khmer. This was the sign of a new age, one in which the Khmer empire, which gradually lost its former hegemony, was in-

creasingly conditioned—on a religious and cultural level—by the neighboring powers. The first of these was Thailand, which in 1350, the year of the foundation of its new capital, Ayutthaya, became a concrete threat for the Khmer, up to the 1431 siege of Angkor Thom and the flight of the city's inhabitants to safer areas. The chronology of the following Khmer kings is uncertain and the historic sources are vague and for the most part were written centuries later. There is no certainty concerning the reasons behind the crisis of the Khmer empire, which in all probability was due to a combination of concurrent causes. The main reason may have been the growing pressure on the part of the Thai, who were in direct contact with the Khmer territories, after centuries of gradual movement from their traditional northern centers to the alluvial plains of central Thailand. The depopulation must have proven fatal to the construction and mainte-

nance of the hydraulic works that were indispensable for the existence of the cities. Growing popular discontent with an authoritarian and spendthrift power system, which had already manifested signs of agitation during the reign of Jayavarman VII, probably continued under his successors, thus contributing to the weakening of the centralized power, which found more and more difficult to control its subject populations. The gradual decrease of the forests, which had provided Angkor with raw material for construction and for everyday needs, is often considered another cause of the regression of the empire. The possible agricultural crisis due to climatic changes is also one of major causes listed by scholars. Proof of this latter theory would be the increase of the diplomatic missions to the Chinese Empire from the end of the 13th century to the first decades of the 14th century, which would suggest the search for new commercial outlets and trade routes.

The creation of Phnom Penh in southern Cambodia, which was in a favorable position for commercial activity, was probably linked to these needs, more so than the quest for an alternative to Angkor, exposed to danger. The Angkor period ended with the emigration of most of the Khmer people from Angkor first in 1432 to Basan, on the left bank of the Mekong River, and then southward, with the establishment of new provisional capitals at Lovek in the 16th century and Udong in the 18th century. Yet the ancient capital was temporarily the seat of the Khmer court between the 16th and 17th centuries, and the preservation of its temples and monasteries was partly due to the almost continuous presence of monastic communities at least throughout the 16th century. In 1434 Phnom Penh took in the first exiles who fled from Angkor and became increasingly important, until it was finally made the capital of the new Cambodian kingdom.

# 4

# THE PERIOD OF DECLINE AND THE MEMORY OF A GREAT PAST

As we have seen, the death of Jayavarman VII was followed by a long period of decline for the Khmer empire that led to its demise as a major political entity in the 14th century. There were many reasons for this development. The Thai became a constant threat along the western border, and Theravada Buddhism (which, with its belief in an austere life and salvation through personal sacrifice, became very popular among the people) soon became a formidable rival of Mahayana, which was favored at the court and was the basis of royal power.

In 1353 the Thai conquered Angkor, which the Khmer reconquered but then lost again, as the city was sacked and burned many times. The northern provinces of the empire (now part of present-day Laos) were lost to Lan Xang, but the deathblow was the Siamese capture of Angkor Thom in 1431. The Angkor region, now depopulated and unsafe, lost the privilege of being the Khmer capital, except for a brief period in the late 16th century. Art also passed through an inexorable decline, for various reasons. The first of these was the impossibility, given the circumstances, of having a steady supply of material from the stone quarries on the foothills, which were dozens of miles away from the city. The second factor was the relative poverty of the kingdom. Consequently, from the 15th to the 17th century most Cambodian sculpture was made of wood, which means that few works have survived, given the perishable nature of this material and the climate of the region. The originality of so much of Indochinese artistic expression therefore

faded away, and later Khmer sculpture betrays a strong Siamese influence. Thus, the residential areas, palaces, temples and other monuments that had constituted one of the most splendid capitals of the past fell into decay, the huge edifices became the home of monkeys and bats, and the extraordinary architecture began to be suffocated by thick forest vegetation that ended up covering it completely.

In the post-Angkor period, during which the political focal point of what remained of the Khmer empire shifted rapidly to the south of the country, to Phnom Penh, there was an inevitable cultural decline. In the following centuries the grandeur of Angkor was a sort of background to the reality of Khmer life. But the local art, now deprived of its traditional patrons and considered secondary because of the needs of a weak and jeopardized kingdom, and soon flanked by European art "imported" for the most part by the French, lost its originality and creative momentum. Then came the time of capitulation to European dominion, the annexation to the French Protectorate of Indochina in 1863. It must be said, however, that this domination prevented the probable dismemberment of the country to the advantage of Siam and Vietnam, and did not obliterate the memory of the extraordinary Khmer civilization. On the contrary, the attraction of exotic art and the need to become acquainted with and organize the colonial territories led to renewed interest in the past: the ancient Khmer monuments and texts were recovered, studied and preserved.

195 - THIS STONE HEAD OF BUDDHA (H. 34 IN.), WHICH WAS SCULPTED IN THE 15TH-16TH CENTURY, STILL HAS TRACES OF COLOR (MUSÉE GUIMET, PARIS).

196 AND 197 - A 15TH-16TH-CENTURY WOODEN STATUE (H. 36 IN.) OF A HIGH-RANKING PERSON PRAYING (NATIONAL MUSEUM, PHNOM PENH).

198 - This 15th-century bronze lion, sculpted in the 'post-Bayon' style (h. 9.5 in.), still has almost all its original gilding (Musée Guimet, Paris).

199 left - A post-Angkorian statue of a dancer refers to the image of the *yakhsas*, the benevolent giants in Hindu mythology (National Museum, Phnom Penh).

199 right - Influenced by neighboring cultures, in the post-classical age Khmer art acquired new forms and materials, such as ceramics. This vase (h. 21 in.) dates from the 13th-14th century (Musée Guimet, Paris).

# THE REDISCOVERY

The ruins of Angkor, "rediscovered" in 1960 by the French naturalist and explorer Henry Mouhot, as well as the remains of the Cham kingdom in Vietnam, brought to light in 1885, are examples–perhaps the most important ones–of a revival of Indochinese tradition. The new techniques of recovery and restoration, together with photography and more efficient preservation and cataloguing systems, improved the possibility of documenting ruins that had been considered lost for ever. The French colonial government established museums and financed archaeological research, while artists, adventurers and art dealers discovered in long-forgotten Angkor a wellspring of inspiration, attraction and business deals. Thus, while on the one hand the past of an entire subcontinent was gradually being reassessed as an instrument of colonial domination, an incitement for dreamlike exoticism and the basis of rapacious art-collecting, on the other hand it also became the foundation of a new-born nationalism that, unable to come to terms with a past that was so difficult to integrate into the present, achieved its "catharsis" by means of the destructive fury of the Khmer Rouge. The Angkor period, the one that marked the apogee of Khmer history, has left over one thousand ancient monuments of different sizes made of stone, and important bas-relief sculptures that tell us so much about court life as well as the daily life of the "commoners," along with the religious practices and beliefs and arts such

as dance and music. The archeological area abounds in images of musical instruments such as the harp (*pinn*), the single-string lute (*khsae muoy*), oboe (*sralay*), crescent gong (*peat*), gong (*korng*), kinds of cymbals (*chhap* and *chhing*), and percussion instruments (*skor*), all of which are still used with modern improvements. All this leads one to believe that the modern Cambodian musical tradition derived from that of the Khmer and is even the art form practiced (or better, revived) that is most directly connected to the ancient empire. This is true in the case of the artifacts made of bronze, brass, copper and iron (or their alloys), which are better preserved and have been perpetuated in Cambodian tradition, both religious and secular.

200-201 - In 1880, Louis Delaporte published the reconstruction of Angkor Wat, together with other views of the site, in his book *Voyage au Cambodge: L'Architecture Khmer*.

201 top - The members of the Mekong Exploration Commission in the ruins of Angkor in June 1866: Doudart de Lagrée's expedition was the first to make systematic surveys of the area.

# A HERITAGE FOR HUMANITY

In the year 2005 more than 1,000,000 people visited the temple complex of Angkor, and this figure is bound to increase in the future. There are many misgivings about this intensive exploitation of an archaeological site that is both fragile and already greatly deteriorated due to illegal digs, pillaging, and land mines, but the need to preserve this great heritage must come to terms with the many needs of a poor country that depends on tourism as a vital source of income and foreign currency. One of the most impressive temples, Phnom Bakheng, seriously risks collapse because of the damage wrought by the excessive number

of visitors (at least 3,000) who climb up to the top every evening to admire the sunset. Be that as it may, the story of Angkor, which in 1992 was one of the 788 sites placed on the UNESCO World Heritage List, marks the success of archaeology and international commitment to the preservation of the past. The task lying ahead—the excavation and preservation of the Khmer sites—is still immense despite the great efforts already made that have gradually extended to embrace regions quite distant from the Angkor area, in both Cambodia and Thailand. But obviously this effort at recovery must involve first and foremost the Cambodians themselves, who are the direct heirs of the Khmer civilization. It is they who are the living link between the past and future—albeit with all the contradictions and terrible poverty that reigns in present-day Cambodia and that will probably characterize the country for quite some time. However, what remains of the ancient Khmer civilization is by rights also the heritage of humanity, so that any commitment and effort to preserve it must involve everyone. The civilization that revolved around Angkor is gradually opening its doors once again to the world, with various objectives that in any case must not ignore the needs (including the contingent ones) of the local population, and with a great amount of compromises and mediation. At the same time, this civilization has become a model laboratory in which new techniques of inspection, survey, excavation, restoration and

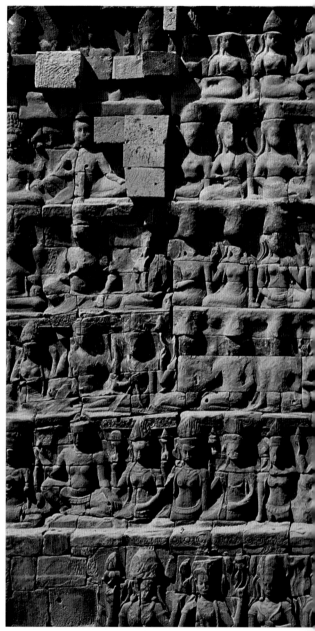

preservation are being experimented. And like all experiments, some have failed or have become mere ends in themselves. It is only natural and legitimate to ask whether all this enormous effort to recover monumental complexes is worthwhile, since the greed, selfishness and ignorance of generations have virtually emptied them of all their artifacts, statues, bas-relief cycles and frescoes, which are now either scattered throughout the world or have been destroyed. Within the limits of its humble dignity,

the National Museum of Phnom Penh houses too many copies of lost masterpieces, too many dusty and often minor residues of a world of incomparable grandeur–a collection that only makes one regret the loss of the magnificence that once existed and will never return. At the same time, the museum is a tangible sign of a small and proud nation's desire for normality and of the possibility of saving for all humanity at least the impressions of what was once a great empire.

202 LEFT AND 203 CENTER AND BOTTOM - FREEING THE EDIFICES OF TA PROHM FROM THE ROOTS OF THE TREES, WHICH HAVE BY NOW BECOME AN INTEGRAL PART OF THE STRUCTURES, WOULD ALSO MEAN ELIMINATING WHAT REMAINS OF THE FINE SCULPTURE DECORATION.

202-203 AND 203 TOP - THE RESTORATION WORK AT ANGKOR IS DIFFICULT BECAUSE OF THE AMOUNT OF WORK TO BE DONE, THE FRAGILE BUILDING MATERIAL, AND THE LACK OF STABILITY OF THE EDIFICES, SO THAT COMPLEX AND CAREFUL RECONSTRUCTION IS CALLED FOR.

## GLOSSARY

**Angkor:** city, capital. The word is used to designate the largest Khmer city, situated north of the Tonlé Sap in Cambodia.

**Apsara:** a celestial dancer or nymph.

**Asrama:** a monastery.

**Asura:** a demon with power similar to those of the gods; the expression of evil.

**Banteay:** "citadel" or "fortress"; a temple surrounded by a wall.

**Baray:** a cistern, artificial lake or reservoir.

**Bodhisattva:** a central figure in Mahayana Buddhism: a potential Buddha who forgoes attaining the state of nirvana in order to help others find the path to salvation.

**Chedi:** the *stupa* of the Indian tradition that was originally used to house the ashes of the deceased and later became the tomb with the relics of an important religious or civil figure.

**Deva** or **devata:** a male deity. Its female equivalent, the *devi*, is not very important in the Khmer religion.

**Devaraja:** the god who is king, a manifestation of the king's power as symbolized by the *linga*.

**Dvarapala:** the temple guardian; it may be either a *deva* or an *asura*.

**Garuda:** a divine vulture that is the mount or vehicle of the god Vishnu and a formidale enemy of the *nagas*.

**Gopura:** the entrance pavilion in temple enclosures.

**Hari-Hara:** the combination of the gods Vishnu (Hari) and Shiva (Hara).

**Linga:** the representation of the penis and symbol of Shiva and of the creative energy of the universe.

**Mandara:** the mythological mountain that is the center of the process of creation of the universe (the Churning of the Ocean of Milk).

**Meru:** mythological mountain considered to be the center of the universe and the abode of the gods.

**Naga:** a serpent, as well as an ophic being connected to the primordial cults of the earth. In the Buddhist sphere, the *naga* Mucilinda protects the Buddha in meditation and is depicted with seven or nine heads.

**Phnom:** a hill or mountain.

**Prasat:** a tower or pyramid temple.

**Wat:** Thai word for "temple" or "sanctuary".

## INDEX

**BIBLIOGRAPHY**

ALBANESE, MARILIA, *Angkor, fasto e splendore della civiltà khmer*. Ed. White Star, Vercelli 2002
BRIGGS, LAWRENCE PALMER, *The Ancient Khmer Empire*. White Lotus, Bangkok, 1999
COE, MICHAEL D., *Angkor and the Khmer Civilisation*. Thames & Hudson, London, 2003
DAGENS, BRUNO, *Angkor, la foresta di pietra*. Electa/Gallimard, Trieste, 1995
DUMARÇAY, JACQUES, *Phnom Bakheng. Etude architecturale du temple*. EFEO, Paris, 1971
DUPONT, PIERRE, *La statuaire préangkorienne*. Artibus Asiae, Ascona, 1955
FREEMAN, MICHAEL, *Khmer temples in Thailand and Laos*. River Books Guide, Bangkok, 1996
GARNIER, F., NAFILYAN, G., CRES, C. & NAFILYAN, J., *L'art khmer en situatione de réserve - Khmer art in reserve*. Editions Européennes, Marseille-Provence, 1997
GITEAU, MADELINE, *Khmer Sculpture and the Angkor Civilization*. Thames & Hudson, London, 1965
GUILLON, EMMANUEL, *Cham Art*. River Books, Bangkok 2001
JACQUES, CLAUDE, *Angkor*. Bordas, Paris, 1990
JACQUES, C., & FREEMAN, M., *Angkor, cité khmer*. River Books Guide, Bangkok, 2000
MACDONALD, MALCOLM, *Angkor and the khmers*. Oxford University Press, 1990
MAZZEO, D. & SILVI ANTONINI, C., *Civiltà khmer*. In: "Le grandi civiltà", Arnoldo Mondadori, Milan, 1972
RAY, NICK, *Cambodia*. Lonely Planet, 2005
ROONEY, DAWN, *Angkor, an Introduction to the Temples*. Odyssey Publications, Hong Kong, 2003
ROVEDA, VITTORIO, *Khmer Mythology. Secrets of Angkor*. River Books, Bangkok, 1997
STERN, PHILIPPE, *Les monuments du style khmer du Bayon et Jayavarman VII*. Presses universitaires de France, Paris, 1965
STERN, PHILIPPE, *Le Bayon d'Angkor et l'évolution de l'art khmer*. In: "Annales du musée Guimet, Bibl. de vulgarisation", t. 47, Librairie orientaliste P. Geuthner, Paris, 1927
STIERLIN, HENRI, *Angkor, Architecture Universelle*. Office du Livre, Fribourg, 1970
STIERLIN, HENRI, *Le mond d'Angkor*. Princesse, Paris, 1979
VANN, MOLYVANN, *Les cités khmer anciennes*. Toyota Foundation, Phnom Penh, 1999
ZÉPHIR THIERRY, *Khmer. Lost empire of Cambodia*. Thames & Hudson, London 1998

**Stefano Vecchia** graduated in Japanese Language and Literature at the University of Turin, and subsequently earned a diploma in oriental languages and culture at the Italian Institute for Africa and the East (IsIAO). He has worked as a professional journalist since 1990, and has divided his time between journalistic work in Italy and trips to Asia, where he is currently a correspondent for Italian publications. He has been chief editor of the magazine *Popoli*, published in Milan, and has been the director of the Milan-based magazine *Quaderni Asiatici* (Asian Notebooks) and manager of the Asia News agency, the first Italian agency reporting only on Asian lands and people. Stefano Vecchia's numerous reports and special photo shoots, published in a variety of journals, are the result of tireless travel and intense professional activity. In 2006 he contributed articles about Japanese and South-East Asian art for "The Great Story of Art" series, published by the newspaper *Il Sole 24 Ore*; and in 2007 he completed guides to Bali and to Japan.

AUTHOR

PHOTO CREDITS

208 - REPRESENTATION OF ELEPHANTS ON THE FAÇADE OF THE TERRACE OF THE ELEPHANTS. THE IMAGES ARE ALMOST LIFE-SIZE AND HAVE AN ABUNDANCE OF DETAILS.